GREYHOUND RACING TO WIN

Victor Knight

GREYHOUND RACING TO WIN

HIGH STAKES

This edition published in 2003 by
High Stakes Publishing
21 Great Ormond St
London WC1N 3JB
T: 020 7430 1021
www.highstakes.co.uk

www.gamblingbooks.co.uk/publishing

ISBN 1 84344 005 9 Greyhound Racing To Win

Printed by Cox & Wyman

Dedication

To my Dad, long gone now but who introduced me to the dogs at Hackney Wick and Walthamstow many years ago. Even today I look for traps 1 and 4!

Acknowledgements

With grateful thanks to the thousands of greyhounds that have given me so much pleasure over the years. Also, to all the punters whose bits and pieces of conversation along the way gave me the basis for much of the advice that follows in this book.

Contents

Greyhound Racing

GREYHOUND RACING is one of the most popular spectator sports in Great Britain, Ireland, Australia and the USA, as well as many other places in the world. Every day of the week many thousands of people pay a visit to their local greyhound track.

The sport is hugely popular for two main reasons. Firstly it is very exciting to watch and makes a great night out. Secondly, it is an excellent betting medium. However, despite it being so good to bet upon, many greyhound fans still lose money. Of course, some people do win but on the whole greyhound punters lose because they fail to appreciate some of the more basic things about the sport. This is where this book will be able to help.

In this book you will learn all about betting on greyhounds. Among many other things, you will find out about the basics of the sport and how important they are to consider when trying to find winners. You will also find out why many punters lose money and what you can do to avoid joining them. Advice will be given on how to rate the form of a race and then how to read that form so you can find the most likely winner.

To win money on greyhound racing you will also need to understand the importance of betting to a plan and taking the long-term view. *Greyhound Racing To Win* aims to help you here as well.

In summary, whether you are a newcomer to betting on the sport or already very experienced, this book will help set you on the way to becoming a winning greyhound race punter.

Greyhound Racing in Great Britain

TODAY, greyhound racing is reported to be Great Britain's second most popular spectator sport (obviously, football is the first). From Monday through to Saturday tracks stage meetings all over the country. A handful race on Sundays as well. Wherever you are in the country there will be a track not too far away. For example, in Scotland there is Glasgow's Shawfield and then right around the country, down to Hove on the south coast near Brighton, tracks are dotted everywhere.

Racing takes place over a variety of distances, over hurdles, and on two types of surface. Nowadays, most tracks are all sand because this kind of surface is easier to maintain. A handful of tracks do still race on grass but all of them have sanded bends. Meetings take place throughout the year and in most weathers. In fact, many of the top tracks have undersoil heating so that even frost and snow cannot prevent racing going ahead. Greyhound race meetings can be anything from 8 to 14 races long.

As well as racing in the evenings, many tracks put on afternoon meetings. Almost all of these are primarily staged for the country's betting shops. These BAGS (Bookmakers Afternoon Greyhound Service) meetings do not attract much in the way of attendance but are seen and bet upon by thousands of betting shop punters. Indeed, some of the dogs that race at tracks where afternoon racing is regularly staged become real favourites in the shops. Many people are critical of BAGS meetings saying the quality of racing is poor, but *Greyhound Racing To Win* will show you that sometimes this criticism is not justified.

At the tracks, punters can bet either with the bookmakers or with the totalisator. At some smaller meetings, the track bookies will not be able to take big bets because the general market will be too weak. But at the large tracks, particularly the London ones, punters will be able to bet in bigger amounts. The size of the track and the number of people attending it will also affect the amounts in the different totalisator pools.

All tracks are equipped with some form of mechanical lure. There are a number of different ones in use but all do the same job, that of enticing the greyhounds to race. Another thing all tracks have in common is that the dogs always race anti-clockwise, i.e. from left to right and all tracks have left-handed bends.

Greyhounds start racing at quite an early age, the minimum is 15 months, and can go on competing until they are around 5, or even 6, years old. That said, most greyhounds reach their peak at about three years of age. Both dogs and bitches race but bitches generally have slightly longer careers. This is because they have an enforced lay-off whenever they come into season. A breeding career will follow for any good class greyhound that has proved itself on the track.

A Brief History of British Greyhound Racing

THE FIRST OFFICIAL RACE MEETING in Great Britain took place on 24 July 1926. It was held at Belle Vue, Manchester but only 1,600 spectators turned up to watch. This was disappointing for the organisers because whippet racing had long been popular, particularly with the miners of Lancashire, Yorkshire and Derbyshire. Furthermore, instances of meetings where greyhounds had chased mechanically driven lures had been recorded as early as 1876.

But the initial disappointment over the first meeting was soon forgotten as, by the end of 1926, some 30,000 people were regularly attending Belle Vue to watch the racing. From there dog racing went from strength to strength and grew quite rapidly. Tracks opened everywhere and the sport enjoyed some wonderful times over the next three decades.

Unfortunately, the 1960s and 1970s saw greyhound racing suffer a long decline during which many tracks closed. At one point the outlook for the sport was very bleak but things have improved over recent years. Although tracks still close from time to time, crowd numbers have stabilised and afternoon BAGS meetings provide a welcome income for many stadiums.

The NGRC (National Greyhound Racing Club) is the sport's controlling body in Great Britain. It is responsible for the legal, disciplinary and registration aspects of greyhound racing at all the country's major tracks. Formed on 1 January 1928, the club's original objectives were to develop a uniform basis for the operation of greyhound racing and to also standardise its procedures. The first rules of racing came into being on 23 April 1928. At all NGRC meetings locally appointed NGRC stewards oversee the racing.

Considering the number of meetings that are run, and the large number of dogs registered to race, the amount of dishonesty that takes place is small. Generally speaking, anyone betting on greyhound racing will receive an honest run for his or her money.

How Greyhound Racing Works

GREYHOUND RACING is a very simple sport. The dogs chase a mechanically driven lure and the first over the finishing line at the end of the race wins. Greyhounds can be disqualified for fighting other dogs in a race but for betting purposes the result will remain the same. It is the way races are put together that makes greyhound racing such a popular pastime.

In Great Britain the vast majority of races consist of six dogs. Some tracks do stage eight dog contests and, in one or two places, only five dogs make up a race. Overall, though, six dog races are the norm. Most greyhound races will fall into one of two categories. They will either be *graded* races or *open* races.

Types of Racing

Most major tracks employ on contract a number of licensed trainers. As part of their contract these trainers have to supply a certain number of greyhounds for racing each week. Some of the very top stadiums employ up to ten trainers for this purpose.

The vast majority of these greyhounds will race only at the track where their trainer is employed. Because of this, a track's racing manager will be able to build up knowledge of the dogs and their different abilities. He or she will keep detailed records of each greyhound's racing career and will use this to put together competitive races. Each of these races will be given a grade by the racing manager according to the level of ability the dogs contesting it are currently showing. Hence the term *graded* racing. The measurement of grades takes place using a simple numbering system. The lowest grade races will generally be 8, 9 or 10 (according to how many dogs are available to race at a track) while the highest grade will be 1. This measurement of each dog's current ability – or form as it is best known – is one of the most appealing things about greyhound racing.

Open races are different from graded ones and are normally contested by dogs that have slightly more ability. Most tracks stage open races on a regular basis. As the name implies, open races are open to all grades of dogs, good or bad, from any track and the race itself is not graded by anyone.

Even greyhounds that normally contest only graded races can run in open races. However, because the prize money is generally greater for open races only the better types of greyhounds normally contest them.

All the major competitions in greyhound racing are open to all dogs. These big competitions can make very attractive betting vehicles but a drawback with open races can occur when one dog is so superior to its opponents it looks almost certain to win. Of course, they don't all do so but beforehand the odds on offer are often unattractive. On the whole, graded races are the best to bet upon and the selection methods later in the book are for use on this type of racing.

Apart from graded and open races, there are two other types of racing. There are *puppy* races and *handicaps,* although both are really just different forms of graded racing. A number of tracks put on contests for young dogs that are relatively new to racing. These puppies will quickly go on to take part in full-blooded graded racing but are often given a slightly more gentle introduction to competition through puppy contests.

Handicaps are races where dogs of different grades compete against each other. The difference in ability is evened out with the less able animals being given starts of varying degrees. For example, if a handicap race is going to be run over 600 metres only the dog or dogs thought to have the most ability will actually run the full distance. The other animals will run slightly less by starting at points further down the track. As the lure passes the dog receiving the longest start, the traps open and the race is underway. Handicaps do not form a major part of racing in Great Britain but can be a very exciting spectacle as the best dogs strive to catch those that have started in front of them.

Distances

Both graded and open races take place over a variety of distances. Some races are as short as 200 metres while others can be up to 1,000 metres and, very occasionally, beyond. However, the majority of races are run over distances between 400 and 650 metres. The 'standard' distance race at almost every track consists of 4 bends. Among the major venues, Crayford in London has the shortest standard distance race of 380 metres, while Hove has the longest with a 515 metres trip. A handful of races take place over hurdles. Depending on the distance of the race, the dogs will jump between 4 and 8 obstacles. Again, this can be a very exciting sight as the dogs skim across the hurdles at close to top speed.

Times

For punters, times are the very backbone of greyhound racing. Every occasion dogs race their times are recorded and so punters have a super guide to how they have been performing. Many punters fail to appreciate just how good a form guide recent times are. Later on in the book, you'll see some simple ways in which recent times can be quantified to show quickly the greyhounds that have been running the fastest.

At many tracks, race times are adjusted by something called a going allowance. This is where the racing manger assesses how much quicker or slower than normal the state of the track surface is allowing the dogs to run. Because the times given on racecards have already undergone adjustment there will be little need to mention going allowances again in this book.

Trials

Before greyhounds can start to race they must first undergo something called trials. Trials are simply where greyhounds run over the distance of a race in order to have their times recorded. From these times racing managers can obtain an idea of a dog's current ability. This is especially important for dogs just starting their racing careers.

Usually, only two, three or four dogs contest a trial, but solo trials where a single greyhound chases the lure are not uncommon either. Trials are not only used for dogs just starting their racing careers though.

Greyhounds returning after a lay-off are normally put through trials before competing in a race. In fact, under the rules of racing any dog that has not raced for over a certain period of time must be 'trialled' before it returns.

Trap Draw

All greyhound races are started through the participants being placed into starting traps. These traps are joined together to form a single unit that can be quickly removed from the track once a race is underway. Although the unit is joined together, each individual trap can still only house one greyhound. Trap 1 is always nearest to the inside of the track and trap 2 next nearest with 6 being on the outside.

The dog in trap 1 wears a red jacket, trap 2 blue, trap 3 white, trap 4 black, trap 5 orange and trap 6 black and white stripes.

The trap draw is one of the most important things in greyhound racing. Under the rules of the sport any greyhound which has shown a tendency to run wide at the bends must be allocated an outside trap (on the racecard wide runners have a W next to their name). This is important because a dog that tried to run wide from an inside trap could cause chaos at the bends. However, a problem with dog racing is that many greyhounds do run wide. Therefore, not all wide running animals end up in the very outside traps.

Wide runners do not usually present a problem in graded racing because racing managers generally try to compile contests where little trouble will occur. (Trouble is the general name given to the bumping, baulking and scrimmaging that can happen between the dogs in a race.) But sometimes racing managers can only find a limited number of dogs with similar ability. In these cases there might be more wide running dogs in a race than would be ideal. This is when punters must carefully consider what might happen in a contest and also why the trap draw is so important when trying to find winners.

Railers are dogs that prefer to race very close to the rails and they will often find themselves in the lower numbered traps. Obviously, this will be to avoid the havoc that could occur if a dog which prefers the rails tries to make its way there from the outside of the track. On an annual basis, trap 1 wins the highest number of races at the majority of venues.

In graded racing, trap allocation is at the discretion of the racing manager but in open races it is generally the subject of a draw that works in the following way. Prior to the draw, the trainers will say whether they want their dogs seeded as either Railers (R), Middle Runners (M) or Wide Runners (W).

Then, the first drawn Railer gets trap 1, the next trap 2, etc. In conjunction, the first drawn Wide Runner gets trap 6, the next 5, and so on. Lastly, the first drawn Middle Runner gets trap 3, the next trap 2 – all subject to availability depending on the other dogs already drawn. The latter is different from graded racing where only Wide Runners are officially seeded. This is why punters need to consider carefully the draw in open races because there is the potential for more trouble as dogs can end up running from unsuitable traps.

Racing Managers

Racing managers probably hold the most important job in the sport. As you have already read, these individuals will compile the graded races at their tracks through looking to match together dogs of similar ability. They will also decide which traps the dogs run out of as well as helping to oversee the racing at each meeting.

Nowadays, almost all racing managers use computer technology to keep a record of each dog's racing career. In the past, though, they used to carry out this task by hand. It also used to be the fashion for racing managers to compile race meetings in a certain way.

About a third of the races at a meeting used to contain a dog that seemingly had a really good chance of winning. This was because bigger punters used to like having dogs to bet upon that would be at fairly short odds but had solid chances of winning. On the other side of the fence, the bookies liked this as well. They would enjoy taking sizeable bets in the hope the dogs would be beaten.

Another third of the races would be compiled so that they seemed to lie only between three or four dogs. Here the betting would be fairly open and so more cash would be bet on the track's totalisator. Finally, the remaining third of the races would be very difficult to solve. This would lead to the betting on these races being very open. Big punters would not be interested but plenty of money would be bet on the totalisator.

Today, cards are not compiled in this way as much as they used to be. However, it is still not uncommon for racing managers to put into the last race of a meeting a dog that has a really obvious chance of winning. The thinking is that many punters will feel inclined to bet on such a dog and, providing it wins, should go home happy and more prepared to pay a return visit to the track. Naturally, they don't all win but over a period of time enough do to justify this way of ending a meeting.

One of the secrets of successful greyhound race betting is to get to know how a track's racing manager works. Armed with this kind of knowledge, punters will soon start to see how races have been put together and when certain dogs have been given particularly good chances of winning.

2nd Race 07.39 pm (Grade A2) **385 Metres Flat**

1st £65; 2nd £22; Others £19

1 Messrs W.Catchesides & S.Gammin Steve Gammon

Hideaway Molly

Red

(Season Unknown) bebd b Deenside Spark – Ballygarron Lady Aug 97 Ir

17 Ap 385	1	04.03	2555	5th	4	Springville Arda	EP,Crowded1&3	24.35	-10	30.35/2J	A2	24.57
11 Ap 415	2	05.00	4344	4th	5	Not Me (Harlw)	Crowded3	26.22	N	30.09/2	OR	26.67
04 Ap 415	4	04.81	1233	4th	7	Lonely Boy (Harlw)	EP, Crd3	26.22	+20	30.110/1	OR	26.60
02 Ap 385	1	04.03	5444	3rd	3½	Frisco Ross	Saw,Rls,RanOn	24.15	-10	29.82/1F	A2	24.37
17 Mr 385	1	03.86	1111	2nd	½	Carriglea Tex	EP,LedToNrLn	24.27	-5	30.05/2	A2	24.26

Figure 1: A Typical Race Card

17Ap 385	1	04.03	2555	5th	4	Springville Arda	EP, Crowded1&3	24.35	-10	30.3	5/2J	A2	24.57	o
a	b	c	d	e	f	g	h	i	j	k	l	m	n	o

Figure 2: The most recent line of form for a dog

The Racecard

MOST GREYHOUND RACECARDS contain a tremendous amount of information. Because there is so much data they can look confusing. Figure 1 (previous page) shows a typical example of how the form for one dog might be laid out. Here are the explanations of what it all means:

2nd Race 7:39 pm: The number of the race at the meeting and time the race is due off.

(Grade A2) 385 Metres Flat: This indicates the grade of the race and that it is a 385 metres long race on the flat (no hurdles)

1st £65 etc: This indicates the prize money on offer to the owners of the dogs in the race.

1 Red: This is the trap number and the colour of the jacket the dog running from it will wear.

Hideaway Molly: This is the name of the dog.

Messrs W.Cathesides & S Gambin: The dog's owners.

Steve Gammon: The dog's trainer.

(Season Unknown): This indicates that the greyhound's last time in season is unknown (something restricted to bitches).

Bebd b Deenside Spark – Ballygarron Lady Aug 97: This tells you the colour of the dog is beige and brindled (Bebd) and that it is a Bitch (b). The next two names, separated by the hyphen, are the sire and the dam of the dog respectively. The Aug 97 is when the dog was born in Ireland (Ir).

Figure 2 (previous page) shows the most recent line of form for the dog:

(a) This indicates its last race was on the 17th April.

(b) 385 was the distance of the race in metres.

(c) The 1 indicates the trap the dog ran from.

(d) The 04.03 was the time in seconds the dog took to go from the traps to the winning line first time around. Known as the sectional time.

(e) 2555 tells you the positions the dog held at the start, ¼, ½ and ¾ points in a race. Known as the sectional placings, or positions.

(f) 5th indicates the dog eventually finished fifth

(g) Distance in lengths the dog finished behind the winner

(h) The winner's name (or the name of the dog that came 2nd if the dog in question won)

(i) The next few words indicate what happened to the dog during the race – in this example EP Crowded1&3 meant the dog showed early pace and was crowded at the 1st and 3rd bends. These are generally known as the 'race remarks'.

(j) The time in seconds the dog that won the race actually recorded.

(k) The going allowance.

(l) The dog's weight (in kilos) before the race.

(m) The dog's odds for the race. She was 5/2 and joint favourite (J)

(n) The grade of the race.

(o) The time Hideaway Molly was calculated as having run in the race.

You can see from just this small example how much information greyhound punters are provided with. The next four lines are the greyhound's four previous races. Two were at another track, Harlow (Harlw), in Open races.

The Best Betting Medium

ARGUABLY, greyhound racing is the very best betting medium of all. To start with, the majority of races have only 6 runners (8 in the USA and up to 10 in Australia). This is surely better than some horse races where 30 or more runners go to post. As well as this, in many races some of the greyhounds can easily be eliminated from consideration because they are clearly out of form. In these cases that can leave only three or four dogs to try to find the winner from. Admittedly, the odds on offer might not always be that long, but one winner at 6/4 is far better than any number of losers at 33/1.

There are many greyhound races where the odds on offer are a genuine reflection of the chances of the runners. At a lot of tracks, 3/1 can be easily obtained about greyhounds that will have a good chance of winning. Not only will they have a good chance of winning, but that chance will not be too difficult to work out. So, on the whole, punters betting with the track bookies will be able to obtain decent odds.

This is not always the case with the totalisator. When a meeting only attracts a small attendance the amount of money bet on the Tote will be low. All tracks take as profit a certain percentage out of their totalisator pools and sometimes this will not leave much remaining. On these occasions the payouts for the winners will often be distorted – especially if the winning dog was the favourite.

Information

Another exciting aspect of greyhound racing is how the facts and figures for every greyhound's performance are recorded and documented. This does not only apply to races but trials as well. What it means is that punters have a mountain of information to help them – probably more so than in any other betting sport. Unfortunately, many punters fail to take advantage of all this information because they do not organise themselves to study it properly. Later on some methods to overcome this problem will be described.

No Jockeys

For many punters, one of the most frustrating things about betting on horse racing is how the jockeys appear to make so many mistakes. Obviously, in many cases at least, it's not the jockeys that have led to punters backing losers but simply that the wrong horses have been selected. However, in greyhound racing there are no jockeys. The performance of each dog cannot be affected by anybody once a race is underway.

Form Assessed

A final advantage of greyhound racing is also a major one. As you will have already seen, the racing manager has a very important role within the sport. The importance of this role cannot be underestimated. Putting it simply, as far as winner finding is concerned the racing manager does much of the work. This comes about through the form of each dog being so carefully monitored.

A racing manger will have an extensive knowledge of each dog's ability and current form. They need to have this in order to put together competitive races. Because each race is given a grade, punters have something to judge the form of the dogs by. Actually printed on the racecard will be the grade of the race under consideration as well as the grade of the races all the dogs have recently been competing in. Of course, in many cases, dogs will come from a grade of race similar to the one they are now in. But if they haven't it will be there on the racecard for everyone to see.

Having the form already assessed and graded by the racing manager gives punters something to judge their reading of it by. A punter may have been carefully watching the recent performances of one particular dog. The occasion may then arrive when the dog is put into a grade of race that the punter believes is wrong.

For example, a punter may believe a dog has been performing to a grade 6 standard. At one meeting the dog may then be dropped into a grade 7 race. Straight away the punter will know the dog may well be better than the standard of race it is in. Naturally, the punter will have to make sure the other dogs in the race do not also possess a grade 6 level of form, but if they don't a good betting opportunity might have arisen. The advantage of having the form pre-graded will then be obvious.

Greyhound Racing in the USA

GREYHOUND RACING in the United States is quite similar to that in Great Britain, but there are some important differences. To start with, the standard number of runners is eight and not six. The trap 1 dog wears a red jacket, trap 2 blue, trap 3 white, trap 4 green, trap 5 black, trap 6 orange, trap 7 green and white, and trap 8 black and yellow.

Another major difference is that there are no track bookmakers, all betting taking place through the totalisator. Also, off course betting in America is illegal in many states and so the crowd numbers at greyhound tracks are considerably higher than in Great Britain.

All tracks are left-handed and the greyhounds chase a mechanical lure. Races are graded in much the same way as Great Britain with dogs moved up and down the grades according to their level of form. Here, though, there is a slight difference in how things are done. In the United States greyhounds are moved up and down the grades according to a set pattern. This pattern is linked to how the greyhounds have been performing.

When a greyhound begins its racing career, it is classified as a maiden (non-winner). When it wins it goes up to a grade D race. Following a win in grade D, it goes to grade C and so on until it reaches the top of the ladder which is grade A. Going the other way, if a greyhound fails to come in first, second or third in three starts, or does not achieve better than two thirds in four starts, it drops down a grade. Depending on the individual state or track, there are also a number of other rules in the United States concerning the way greyhounds must be moved up and down the grades according to how they have been performing. In the United States, the grading of greyhounds is known as handicapping.

In Great Britain, the racing manager generally upgrades dogs that win, but not automatically so. If the racing manager sees fit to leave the greyhound in the same grade of race it has just won in, they can. Alternatively, the dog could be put up two grades if it has had a very impressive win. A further important difference between greyhound racing in the USA and Great Britain is how information is laid out on the racecards. Although the information given serves the same purpose, and is broadly similar, there is a lot more of it on American racecards.

On the racecard, race distances are given in 8ths or 16ths of a mile, or in feet. This is also different from Great Britain where distances are given in metres.

In America greyhound racing is very popular in many states, but none more so than Florida. The Sunshine State can boast of drawing to its 18 tracks a significant percentage of the 20 million plus people who attend the sport in the USA each year.

Greyhound racing started in United States during the early years of the century. As early as 1912 a patent for the invention of a dummy hare had been put forward. The first track was probably opened in California although it was reportedly a crude effort. Following on, another track was built in Tulsa. This was about the time when the First World War ended and the sport soon became very popular.

Within six months of the track opening at Tulsa, a second had been constructed, also in Florida. Soon after the sport was on its way to becoming one of the country's most popular forms of entertainment. Just a few years later it found its way to Great Britain and Ireland.

Today in the USA, greyhound racing is the country's sixth most popular spectator sport. At time of writing it was legal in 18 states: Alabama, Arizona, Arkansas, Colorado, Connecticut, Florida, Idaho, Iowa, Kansas, Massachusetts, Nevada, New Hampshire, Oregon, Rhode Island, South Dakota, Texas, West Virginia and Winsconsin.

As previously mentioned, a feature of greyhound racing in the USA is just how good the racecards are. There is a tremendous amount of information on them and they are a great aid to the vital business of finding winners. Figure 3 (overleaf) shows an example of one dog's formlines. Here is an explanation of what it all means:

Lincoln Downs: Name of the track (Lincoln Downs is in Rhode Island)
05-15a: Time of the race (05:15 in the afternoon)
01: Race number

Lincoln Downs	05-15a	01	M 5-16

1

Mystic Rider	57	Ken Wayne R. Ward	LN 5 0 1 1 1

Trn   Carlos Diaz

R F Sept 1999 Sc's Mask Rider Evening Colors   Owner Wayne R. Ward

Hi Grade – M   Lo Grade – M   Btime – 32.18

05-10a	1	5-16	F	31.43	57 ½	5	3	4	3	2	2	1	31.50	13.10	M	Slight Gain,midtra
05-05e	1	5-16	F	31.45	58	6	8	8	14	6	6	13	32.38	32.00	M	Some Gain,midtra
04-30a	1	5-16	F	31.40	58	3	2	2	6	3	4	5	31.75	5.20	M	Faded
04-20e	2	5-16	F	31.62	57	3	4	4	4	4	3	3	31.83	9.50	M	Ran On
04-12a	1	5-16	F	31.32	58	2	4	5	6	5	7	16	32.50	8.50	M	Faded

Figure 3: A USA dog's formlines

05-10a	1	5-16	F	31.43	57 ½	5	3	4	3	2	2	1	32.18	13.10	M	Slight Gain,midtra
a	b	c	d	e	f	g	h	i	j	k	l	m	n	o	p	q

Figure 4: The most recent line of form for a dog

28

M 5-16: Maiden Race over 5/16ths of a mile
1: Trap Number
Mystic Rider: Dog's name
57: Current weight in lbs
Ken Wayne R. Ward: Name of Kennel
LN 5 0 1 1 1: Racing record of the dog at the track: 5 races, 0=1st, 1=2nd, 1=3rd, 1=4th (only runs in the first four recorded here)
R F Sept 1999 Sc's Mask Rider Evening Colors: Dog's breeding details
Owner: Wayne R. Ward: Dog's current owner
Hi Grade – M Lo Grade – M: Highest grade dog has run in / Lowest grade dog has run in
Btime: Dog's best time

Figure 4 (previous page) shows the most recent line of form for the dog:

(a) 05-10a is Date of Race i.e.: 10th May in the afternoon.
(b) Trap Number
(c) Race distance
(d) Going (F means Fast, M is Muddy, S is Slow)
(e) Winner's time
(f) Weight (in lbs)
(g) Box (trap) position
(h) Start Call (position at opening of traps)
(i) 1/8th Call
(j) Stretch call (position at the straight off the 4th bend, otherwise known as the 'third call')
(k) Finish call
(l) Finishing position
(m) Distance beaten by (or won by)
(n) Dogs Actual Running time (Unlike GB, each dog's time is actually recorded and not calculated. But .07 of a second roughly equates to about 1 length)

(o) Totalisator Odds – declared to, and including, $1 stake
(p) Grade of Race (M equals Maiden)
(q) Race Remarks

The important thing to remember with racecards in the USA is that the information given in the formline does slightly vary from track to track. All tracks have their own 'call positions', although all of them use a Start, 1/ 8th, Stretch and Finish. The best advice upon visiting a new track is to read the card carefully to see what other 'calls' appears in the form lines.

Greyhound Racing in Australia

AUSTRALIANS LOVE greyhound racing and people all across this vast country attend meetings on a regular basis. As a result, four different bodies in four different areas marshal the sport.

To start with, in New South Wales the controlling body is known as the Greyhound Racing Authority, which has 41 racetracks under its jurisdiction. Moving on, Queensland also has a Greyhound Racing Authority that looks after 12 venues. The Western Australia Greyhound Racing Authority looks after the sport at 13 provincial tracks in Victoria as well as two world class venues in Melbourne. Lastly, the GRSA is the controlling body for greyhound racing in South Australia.

With up to 10 dogs contesting each race, the sport in Australia is similar to that in the USA. Races are run over a variety of distances from 274 to 840 metres, and sometimes beyond. Prize money is big in Australia with tracks in Victoria frequently offering feature events where the winning owner pockets $5,000 or $10,000. One difference from the USA, though, is how, like Great Britain, there are track bookmakers as well as the Totalisator.

A negative point about greyhound racing in Australia, however, is that the racecards are generally not as detailed as those in Great Britain and the USA. For example, sectional times are often not given. Also, the tracks within the different governing bodies have different ways of laying out the form. Unfortunately, this makes it hard to illustrate an example.

This is a little disappointing because the sport continues to go from strength to strength in Australia. However, recently there has been some attempt to standardise and improve the presentation of the form across the country, as some investigation on the internet will soon reveal.

Greyhound Racing in Ireland

IN IRELAND, the sport is almost the same as it is in Great Britain. In fact, many of the greyhounds that race in GB come from Ireland for Ireland almost certainly breeds the best racing dogs in the world. From the top-class Shelbourne Park in Dublin – first meeting 14 May 1927 and long home to the Irish Derby – through to smaller country tracks set in some delightful areas, dog fans in Ireland have plenty of places to go and watch their sport. From the first meeting at Celtic Park, Belfast on Easter Monday, 1927 when 3,000 people turned up, the sport has gone from strength to strength.

Indeed, over the past few years greyhound racing has enjoyed a real boom in Ireland and some big money has been pumped into the sport to upgrade the facilities at a number of tracks. The knock-on effect has been an increase in crowd numbers and thus a significant rise in race prize money. Today, the Irish Greyhound Derby is arguably the world's premier dog racing competition.

The majority of greyhound owners in Ireland also supervise the training of them as well. Furthermore, many go on to start up breeding operations and sell the dogs they produce through agents who place them with owners in Great Britain. Like Great Britain, greyhound punters can either bet with on-course bookmakers, or use the track totalisator.

The only thing one could criticise about greyhound racing in Ireland is that some tracks, as in Australia, do not produce racecards as good as those in Great Britain and the USA. For example, most tracks do not give sectional times on their cards. Given the rate of development of the sport in the past few years, this will surely be something the Irish Greyhound Board – Bord na gCon – soon turns its attention to. After all, arguably the best racing greyhounds in the world deserve to have their exploits documented in as much detail as is possible.

The Form

GREYHOUND RACING is all about form. Probably even more so than with horse racing. This is because, to a certain degree, the fitness of a racehorse can be judged through looking at it in the pre-race ring. Horses are large animals and there are things to look for that will tell you the level of fitness they have attained. If nothing else, this will at least give some indication of what might win a race.

With greyhounds, however, it's not so easy. Greyhounds are smaller and do not parade for as long before their races as horses do. Of course, there are ways to tell if a greyhound is fit through its appearance but a far more reliable way of seeing if a dog has any chance of winning is through studying its form.

Unfortunately, for many punters form study is a big problem. This isn't because they don't understand what they are reading – although many misinterpret it – but because they become confused with all the information that is available. The key is to organise the form so it can be studied more easily. In fact, this is one of the most crucial things of all.

Once a method for studying form is adopted many punters start to find winners on a more regular basis. Sometimes, winners even start to jump off the page because the same method of looking at the form is being used race after race. Apart from this, organised form study makes trying to find winners that much more fun. Instead of becoming frustrated and confused by all the different bits of information, punters start to enjoy studying the facts and figures.

When the form is studied in an organised way it will also become clear what information is relevant and what isn't. Furthermore, it will then start to appear obvious how much of the minor, or even irrelevant, bits of form punters latch on to. As a result, you'll realise why so many punters make the same mistakes over and over again.

There is one final and highly important point about organising the form so it's easier to study. Many greyhound racing fans have busy lives. As a result, they have little time to study form. This is made worse when they visit the tracks because there are only short intervals between races. At some evening meetings in Great Britain there is as little as 14 minutes between contests. Ideally the form should have been studied before racing but this is clearly not possible for everyone.

So, to take full advantage of the time that is available, especially at the tracks, an organised method of form study will be very useful. To emphasise this point, next time you are at the track watch your fellow racegoers. It will probably surprise you how many are studying the form in a disorganised manner. (Not to mention latching on to irrelevant bits of it as they do so.) You'll only need to listen to them talking to realise this!

In the next chapter, a number of ways to organise and analyse the form so as to make it easier to study will be discussed. First, though, let's take a look at what constitutes 'form' itself.

What is form? A greyhound's form is a collection of most of the things printed on a racecard. Although there is a lot of information given, for the purposes of form study some bits are more important than others. It's obtaining knowledge of how to read these relevant pieces of form that is one of the keys to finding winners at the dog track. The following factors are almost certainly the most important.

Times

Before looking at how times should be interpreted there is one important thing to note. The winning greyhound in each race or trial has its time recorded in two ways. Firstly, by means of photo- or ray-timing and, secondly, through the use of a hand-held stopwatch. If a fault occurs with the former, the latter is called upon. However, all the other greyhounds in a race or trial have their time calculated.

The calculation is based upon the time of the winning dog. How far behind the winner the other dogs finish dictates the time each of them is credited with. The basis of calculation is as follows:

Short Head:	0.01 of a second.
Head/Neck:	0.02 of a second.
Half a Length:	0.04 of a second.
One Length:	0.08 of a second.

So, if the winner of a race records 30.00 seconds, a dog finishing 1 length behind will be credited with a time of 30.08. Remember, this is how things work in Great Britain. In the US each of the dogs have their time individually recorded.

Initially, it might seem disturbing that calculated times are used for all but the winner of each race or trial, but it isn't a problem. The same method of calculation is used for every dog and this way of doing things has served greyhound racing well for quite a long time.

As already noted, a dog's race time, actual or calculated, is given on the far right-hand side of the racecard. The most recent races are at the top and they then descend in date order. Out of everything else on the card, times are arguably the most important piece of information. Through using times, especially the most recent ones, punters can obtain a pretty accurate picture of which greyhounds are in the best form. Of course, there is more to it than just the clock but times are a great place to start.

Just sometimes, the rest of the information on a card can mask how a greyhound really ran but the times cannot. If a dog finds lots of trouble in a race (trouble is where a dog is baulked, bumped or generally hampered from having a clear run) its time will probably be poor. Alternatively, a dog that produces a good time despite encountering problems in running has probably done well.

Times can also greatly aid form study when a greyhound wins a race by a wide margin, especially if it has done so through missing trouble behind. Unless a punter saw the race they probably won't know why the winning margin was so large. This might lead to the form being overvalued. But here the time the dog recorded will be useful. Through looking at it the punter will know whether the form is going to stand up to closer inspection. Using times in conjunction with the race remarks is an excellent way to see how a greyhound fared during previous contests. Note: a greyhound that has been recording poor times whilst enjoying clear runs will almost certainly be out of form.

Obviously, the faster a time the better, but there's more to it than that. The higher the grade of race a time was set in, the more valuable it will be formwise. If one greyhound has recorded a time of 30 seconds for a grade 3 race but another the same in grade 1, the grade 1 form will probably be slightly better. This is because the dogs running in grade 1 races will be showing better form than those competing in grade 3 (remember, the lower the number the better the grade of race).

Generally speaking, times set in trials will be faster than those recorded in races. The reason for this is obvious. Most trials are made up of fewer dogs than races are. Thus, greyhounds will have more room to run and faster times will be recorded as a result.

An important point about times in Great Britain is that those recorded in the summer are just a fraction more reliable than those set in winter. This is simply because the going in summer, even on sand surfaces, is more stable. The surface remains firmer and greyhounds produce more consistent times. That's not to say in the winter they should be dismissed. Certainly not, but from mid-April through to mid-November times probably stand up to slightly closer inspection.

Fast Times

You would think that the faster a time, the better a greyhound has run. On the whole this is true, but not always so. Sometimes a greyhound will record a fast time simply because it has been 'towed around' behind a very quick winner.

When a dog has been showing little in the way of form but then suddenly comes second or third in a fast time behind a quick winner, be sceptical. Take a careful look at the race comments for the dog. If these tell you the animal enjoyed a clear run throughout, treat the fast time with a little caution. Primarily, most greyhounds like to chase the lure but if they see another dog well in front of them some tend to chase that instead. This is no bad thing but it can mean a 'false' time being recorded. If the dog didn't have another greyhound in front of it to chase it may not have been so keen! So, be aware of 'towed around' times.

Where a fast time can be a valuable piece of information is when a dog produces it after being upgraded. This can often be a sign that a dog is rapidly improving, as it has not only been able to handle its upgrade but return a good time as well. When this happens with a dog under two years old it can be a very positive sign that the animal is going to enjoy a successful racing career.

Slow Times

Alternatively, really slow times generally mean one of three things. As we've already discussed, a slow time could mean a dog found a lot of trouble in its race. Or, it could mean the dog is well out of form. However, there is one final thing applicable only to sanded tracks.

From time to time, sanded racing surfaces are scarified between meetings. This is generally done when the track has become very hard and compacted, something that happens in dry spells. To combat this, a track's racing manager will have the track scarified, which means the sand is loosened without being turned over. As a result, the track will run noticeably slower for a short while. Even though this will be accounted for through the 'going allowance', it can still have a noticeable affect on times.

Grade of Race

The grade of a race is given through a letter and number being attached to it. Because the racing manager classifies each dog's run this piece of information is highly important. Generally speaking, in Great Britain the letter A is usually attached to races over the standard 4 bend distance, such as 400 metres at Romford or 515 metres at Hove. The letter S is also frequently used for the most commonly deployed longer distance trip, which will normally consist of 6 bends – for example, 640 metres at

Walthamstow or 660 metres at Wimbledon.

The figure used alongside the letter indicates the grade of race. As already mentioned, 1 is the highest grade of race (regardless of the distance) and 8, 9 or 10 – occasionally even lower – are the bottom grades.

Race grades tell punters a great deal – providing they interpret them properly. Frequently, dogs that have been downgraded (put into a lower grade of race than they last competed in) have good chances of winning. Of course, not all of them do so but looking for animals racing in lower grades is often a useful place to begin when trying to find winners. However, common sense needs to be applied.

For example, if three or more dogs in a race have been downgraded from their previous contest, the grade of the current race becomes a little irrelevant. In other words, should, say, three or four dogs be put into an A6 race after their last runs were all in A5 grade, the current contest is probably of A5 standard itself. The downgrading will therefore mean very little.

Better to look for races where only one or, at the most, two animals have been downgraded. Then, a betting opportunity might exist. However, more work will still be needed before knowing whether this is the case or not.

When a downgraded dog has been found, look at its most recent form. Should it have clearly been running poorly it may still fail to do much in the lower grade. Sometimes, when dogs are out of form they go down a number of grades before recording another win. But, not infrequently, a dog is downgraded when it has been running well without winning. In Great Britain, racing managers sometimes use this technique to give punters a chance to back a winner. There are no guarantees of course, and not all punters latch onto it, but a dog that has been in reasonable form and is then downgraded can be a good betting proposition.

In the USA, the 'self-grading' technique – remember, greyhounds automatically move up and down the grades according to their performances – means opportunities for punters to land upon a deliberately downgraded dog are not as great. Therefore, it is crucial for punters in the USA to note why a greyhound has been automatically downgraded. They really do need to see if the downgrade is due to repeated bad luck in running rather than because the animal is out of form.

Because greyhounds are automatically downgraded, the reasons for poor performances become all the more relevant. If a dog fails to reach the positions required to remain in its present grade it might be due to a loss of form. This would be illustrated by a dog's race remarks indicating it was enjoying clear runs. Or, it might be because it has been unlucky in running. This would be shown through recent race remarks indicating it was baulked, bumped or hampered. Although the same situation can happen in Great Britain, it's in the USA where close study of the form for any downgraded dogs is particularly important.

Upgraded Dogs

On both sides of the Atlantic, greyhounds that have been upgraded pose punters a problem. Dogs that have been upgraded often fail to reproduce their winning form because they can't cope with the slightly better standard of animals they are asked to compete against. In fact, so many upgraded dogs fail to win in their next race it might be thought worthwhile to steer clear of all of them.

Yet, there are still some animals that do cope with an upgrade and, as a result, put together two, three or – very occasionally – even more wins. It's probably true to say that this happens more with younger dogs, those under two years of age, than with any others.

Another thing to note about upgraded dogs is how they often finish second the first time they tackle a higher grade before going on to score in that same class next time out. Note: the latter probably happens frequently enough for punters to consider very closely any greyhounds entering a race with this kind of form.

Race Remarks

These are the remarks relating to what happened to a dog in each of its races. They are crucial when trying to find a winner and a full list of what they mean is given at the end of the book. Although all remarks are significant, there are some that are more valuable to punters than others.

For example, if a dog has won and the remark describing its running is Qaw, Ald (which means quick away from the traps, always led) you're not told very much. There's nothing wrong with the remark – when a win is achieved in this fashion it's the only description that can be used – but the time the dog has returned for the race will be more important.

However, if a dog has finished close-up in second or third place with the remark Baulked 1, RanOn, it might mean it was an unfortunate loser. Consequently, it might be worthy of consideration next time out. (Baulked 1, RanOn means the dog was prevented from running the course it was trying to take at the first bend but continued to try to run as fast afterwards).

It is the latter kind of remark that is really valuable. When a greyhound has endured a rough ride yet has still managed to finish close up, punters should take note. Use remarks relating to this kind of thing in conjunction with the position a dog held at each of the four sectional points from the race. Should it be clear from this information a dog was at the rear of its field early on, but then still worked its way through to finish second or third, it's generally a positive sign. Even more so if it had to overcome trouble in running.

What punters need to be looking for with race remarks, like the one just described, are indications that a greyhound may have gone close to winning had it not met trouble. Greyhounds that have done this might well produce the goods next time out. As a good example, consider this race remark for a dog's last but one outing at a top London track not very long ago. In this race the dog eventually finished second.

Bmp1, Bmp&Ld3/4-NrLn, Imp

This means the dog was bumped at the first bend, bumped ¾ of the way through the race but at that point also took the lead and held it until near the line when it was impeded. Its position at each of the four sectional points in the race was 4421.

Quite an eventful race for the dog but also a whole load of information for astute punters to go on. Had the dog not been bumped twice and then impeded near the line, might it have won? Despite its fairly rough ride, the dog appears to have continued with its effort. Incidentally, next time out the dog finished an unhampered third in a very quick time before going on to win at odds of 3/1 the race after.

Naturally, finding winners is not always as easy as the last couple of examples may have made it sound. Far from it, but looking for significant race remarks in conjunction with sectional positions, times, and the grade of race the times were achieved in will not see punters go far wrong.

Trap Draw

Not really form as such but certainly part of the picture. Some greyhounds do not like certain traps and will not perform well when running from them. In the Racing Post greyhound section, a table carrying details of each of the runners' racing records accompanies most of the main meetings. This will include the ratio of how many times each dog has won from the trap occupied in the current race. If the ratio is really poor, think twice about backing the dog no matter how good its form and times are. On the other hand, a good ratio of wins from the currently occupied trap is a very positive sign.

Sectional Times

An interesting set of figures that can be very important when reading the form. The sectional time given for each race is simply the time it took the animal to run from the traps to the winning line first time around (second time around in 8 bend races). It is in the standard distance 4 bend races where these times mean the most. In these kind of races (other than at the race end) the dogs only go across the finishing line once. Because of the proximity of the line to the first bend, the sectional times are a good indicator of which greyhound is going to reach that point first – and thus have the best chance of obtaining a trouble free run.

In standard distance 6 bend races, the runners still only cross the winning line once before race end, but after two bends have already been run. Hence, the sectional times are not as valuable for these kinds of races. In marathon races (8 bends or more) the dogs do cross the winning line twice before race end – on both the first and second circuits. Hence, in races of this type, the sectional time given is that achieved as the dogs hit the line second time around. But these figures mean very little because a full circuit will have already been negotiated before the time is recorded. Incidentally, in 2 bend races (rare but far from unheard of) the winning line is only met once, and that is at the finish!

Sectional times can be really helpful when looking for the winner. In the next chapter we will look at how to 'read a race'. The reasons why sectional times are so useful will be discussed then.

Sectional Placings

We've already looked at the main reasons why the sectional placings or positions – call them what you will – are such an important piece of information. Through them it can be seen where a dog lay at four different stages of a race. Note: As much as punters should look closely at dogs that have run well despite having encountered trouble, steer clear of dogs that, in their last race or two, have enjoyed a clear passage but remained at the back of the field for the entire contest. Chances are they will be well out of form.

So, that's a brief look at some of the more relevant pieces of information helping to make up the form of a racing greyhound.

In practice, when studying the form for any race an astute punter will pull together all the information on a card. But by making sure they really concentrate on the things we've just discussed, winner finding will be made much easier.

Analysing the Form and Selection methods

BECAUSE A GREYHOUND'S form is made up of a number of facts and figures it really does help if the most important bits of information are dealt with in a logical way. However, there's more to it than that. If the form is analysed in the right kind of way busy punters, if they want to, will be able to select greyhounds very quickly.

This will apply equally to greyhound racing in Great Britain, the USA, Ireland and Australia. So, the form analysis and selection methods that follow should prove effective either side of the Atlantic.

Recent Form

The most important elements of a greyhound's form are its times, the grade of the races it set the times in, and its finishing positions in those races. As with horse racing, recent form is almost certainly the most valuable. Bearing this in mind, these form analysis & selection methods are all based on very recent form.

The other thing to note about all the methods is that they are designed to work on graded racing only. As greyhound racing is very largely made up of these kinds of contests, this is no problem. Having said that, in Great Britain with big competitions like the Greyhound Derby, almost all of the methods can be used once two rounds of the competition are complete. Indeed, for something like the Greyhound Derby this first method will prove very effective.

Method 1

The first method concentrates upon the two most recent appearances each greyhound has made over the distance of the race now being contested. Different parts of it form the basis for all but one of the other methods as well. It will also demonstrate how simple it is to make the form easier to study.

To use the method effectively, a racecard giving at least two lines of form, preferably three, will be needed. This shouldn't be a problem because all greyhound race stadiums provide cards with a minimum of this amount of form on them. Also, in Great Britain the *Racing Post* provides cards for all the major tracks and these will carry at least two lines of form as well.

Step 1

Go through the form for each greyhound and isolate the times from the two most recent appearances made over the same distance of race as that now being contested. Prefer races to multiple dog trials (where more than one dog has contested the trial) and multiple dog trials to solo trials. Also, do not use any form more than six weeks old. In greyhound racing, form older than this frequently shows itself to be unreliable.

Do bear in mind that occasionally a dog's form will contain only one, or even no, times to isolate. This will happen when a greyhound has not been running regularly over the distance of the race it is now contesting.

Step 2

Once all the relevant times have been isolated, refer to the most recent one for each greyhound. Compare them each to one another and award 6 points to the fastest, 5 points to the next fastest and so on through to 1 point for the slowest. (Here it's worth pointing out that if two dogs have the same time and thus score an equal number of points, the next fastest time will score 1 point less than you may immediately think. i.e. if two dogs are tied on one time and each score 4 points, the next fastest time will earn 2 points, not 3.)

Step 3

Now, repeat step 2 but use the second most recent time for each greyhound.

Step 4

Add up the two sets of points awarded for each dog and write down the six totals.

Step 5:

Now, look at the appearance where each dog achieved its most recent time – the first one isolated in step 1. Take note of the dog's finishing position and the grade of the race. Then, refer to the table below and award points accordingly.

For example, a dog finishing 4th in a grade 5 race would score 10 points.

FINISHING POSITION

RACE GRADE	1st	2nd	3rd	4th	5th	6th
One	17	16	15	14	13	12
Two	16	15	14	13	12	11
Three	15	14	13	12	11	10
Four	14	13	12	11	10	9
Five	13	12	11	10	9	8
Six	12	11	10	9	8	7
Seven	11	10	9	8	7	6
Eight	10	9	8	7	6	5
Nine	9	8	7	6	5	4
Ten	8	7	6	5	4	3
Eleven	7	6	5	4	3	2
Twelve	6	5	4	3	2	1

Note 1: When using this table, treat trial runs in the following manner: Deduct 1 point from the table score for each of the number of greyhounds below six that contested the trial, e.g. a dog finishing 1st in a grade four 3-dog trial would score 14 points from the table (1st in grade 4). But then 3 points would be deducted because 3 dogs less than 6 ran in the trial. So, the final score would be 11 points. Had it been a 2-dog trial, 4 points would have been deducted and so on. **Note 2**: For 8 dog races, simply extend the whole table by two points

Step 6:
Repeat step 5 using the second most recent appearance, the time of which was isolated in step 1.

Step 7
The final step. Total up the figures for each dog awarded in steps 5 and 6. Then, add to the points totalled up from step 4. The greyhound(s) with the highest total almost certainly has the best most recent form.

The highlighted areas in Figure 6 (overleaf) are the ones used in this method.

(1) The two most recent times over the distance of the race in question.
(2) The grade of the races.
(3) The finishing positions.

The points table used in this method is known as the 'Wimbledon system'. A famous racing manager called Con Stevens developed and perfected this method of grading form at the South London track many years ago. By combining the table with points awarded for recent times, a very clear picture of current form can be obtained.

A surprisingly large number of winners will come from the dogs achieving the top two scores. Therefore, if so desired, punters can simply

2nd Race 07.39 pm						(Grade A2)						385 Metres Flat
						1st £65; 2nd £22; Others £19						
1	Hideaway Molly					Messrs W.Catchesides & S.Gambin						Steve Gammon
Red						(Season Unknown) bebd b Deenside Spark – Ballygarron Lady Aug 97 Ir						
17 Ap 385	1	04.03	2555	5th	4	Springville Arda	EP,Crowded1&3	24.35	-10	30.35/2J	A2	24.57
11 Ap 415	2	05.00	4344	4th	5	Not Me (Harlw)	Crowded3	26.22	N	30.09/2	O	26.67
04 Ap 415	4	04.81	1233	4th	7	Lonely Boy (Harlw)	EP, Crd3	26.22	+20	30.110/1	O	26.60
02 Ap 385	1	04.03	5444	3rd	3½	Frisco Ross	Saw,Rls,RanOn	24.15	-10	29.82/1F	A2	24.37
17 Mr 385	1	03.86	1111	2nd	½	Carriglea Tex	EP,LedToNrLn	24.27	-5	30.05/2	A2	24.26

Figure 6: A Typical Race Card showing the areas used in Method 1

back these dogs blindly. As a selection method, this way of 'rating' greyhound from will prove very effective.

But in addition, using this method to organise the form will make it easier to study. Straight away, punters will be able to see the dogs with the best current form as well as those running moderately. As has been pointed out, there are so many bits and pieces of information associated with greyhound racing it can be hard to know where to start when looking for the winner.

Making the form easier to study will assist punters because most will want to use their own judgement in arriving at a final selection for a race. So, assuming a race has been 'rated' using this method, let's look at a few ways to make form studying even more focused.

(1) Eliminate the dogs that have achieved the three lowest scores. Confine your form study to the dogs that remain after the ones with the lowest three scores have been eliminated. It is from these dogs that many winners will come. In fact, regular use of this method will soon allow you to identify the races where some of the dogs can be safely eliminated because they have little chance of winning. It's races like these you should be looking to bet in.

(2) Try to avoid races where there is a tight band of points between the highest and lowest scoring dogs: Races of this kind will probably be tightly graded affairs and, although the odds will reflect the competitiveness of the contest, finding the winner will be hard.

(3) When a dog achieving one of the two highest scores is also downgraded take very careful note: Such animals will always have good chances of winning.

(4) Look closely at any dogs that achieve two sets of 6 points from steps 2 and 3 of the method: Dogs like these will probably have a useful advantage on the clock. If any in this situation have also been downgraded, look closer still. And, in addition, if they are housed in traps 1 or 6 you may well have a real bet on your hands! Why? Simply because they will have almost everything that matters in dog racing going for them. Needless to say, opportunities like this will not come along very often.

(5) Be a little wary of supporting upgraded dogs: We've discussed how upgraded dogs sometimes find it harder to win when they first go into a new grade. So, be careful when considering any dogs that achieve one of the top scores but have been upgraded from their previous contest.

(6) Avoid 'trial' dogs: Although dogs do sometimes win their first race back after a set of trials, on the whole it's probably best to avoid them because their race-fitness will need to be taken on trust. It should never be completely dismissed, but the only time trial form is really useful is when a dog returning to racing, or a new dog, lines up in a low-grade race against some real old plodders. From time to time, every track puts on a very low-grade contest where the majority of the runners have been performing poorly for long periods. Then, a dog fresh from a couple of trials can hold a good chance.

(7) Avoid dogs with the worst B.R.T: The initials B.R.T. stand for Best Recorded Time. Under this heading will be the best time in the past three months each greyhound has recorded over the distance of the race it now contests. It's rare for either of the dogs achieving the best two scores under method 1 to have the worst B.R.T. but if one does it's probably best to steer clear. Dogs with the worst B.R.T. do win but not that often. Also, as a way of helping decide between the dogs with the two or three best scores, the B.R.T. can be useful.

Overall, this first method will be of enormous help. It's a simple idea but simple things are often the best. Used as either a way of analysing the form ready for further study, or as a straightforward selection method, it will surprise you with its effectiveness. At first, it might take a little getting used to, but after a short while you'll be rating races in no time at all. But before we move on to something else, let's look at a modified version. This slightly cut-down version will be quicker to use but is equally effective. However, it will tend to put more dogs on the same scores than the original method. It's still worth looking at though.

Step 1
Same as first method.

Step 2
Same as the first method, but instead of awarding 6 points to the fastest time etc. do the reverse and award points in ascending order, 1 point to the fastest time and so on.

Step 3
Do the same as step 2 but now use the second most recent time.

Step 4
Add the two sets of figures up.

Step 5
Now, look at the races where each dog achieved the times just used and note their finishing positions as well as the grade of the races. Add the four figures up.

Step 6
Finally, add the total from step 6 to the total from step 4.

As an example, if a greyhound has finished 3rd and 4th in its last two races and they were both grade 6 contests, its total will be 3 + 4 + 6 + 6 which is 19.

The lower the score, the better a greyhound's current form. The idea is that the lower the points score from the times section the better the times must be. As well as this, the lower the number of the race grade, the higher class it is and the lower the number of finishing position the better the greyhound ran.

Method 2

The first method will enable you to select a greyhound in almost every race. However, this second method is much more exclusive. In fact, only a small number of greyhounds will meet its criteria but they will be greyhounds with excellent chances of winning. This is because the method concentrates on finding downgraded dogs that have still recorded decent times in their last two races.

Step 1
Look through each race on a card to see if there are any downgraded dogs.

Step 2
Only proceed with races where downgraded dogs are running.

Step 3
For any races with downgraded dogs, use steps 1 through to 4 of the first method.

Step 4
Finally, select any downgraded dogs that achieve a score of 8 points or better.

The idea behind this method is very simple. It illustrates downgraded dogs that have still been returning decent times compared to their opponents. The aim is to avoid greyhounds that have been downgraded just because they are out of form.

This method will not throw up many selections, so it might be thought worthwhile to increase the size of your bets upon them. In the long run, fewer bets with larger stakes are going to prove broadly the same as more bets with smaller stakes

Method 3

This method again uses the two most recent times of each greyhound, but in a slightly different way from the first couple we've looked at. It's a very quick way to see the dogs that have recently been running the fastest. It might be considered suitable as a simple way to initially analyse the form ready for more detailed study.

Before describing the system, there are a couple of points to note.

(1) Do not use any times set more than 42 days ago or outside of a dog's last five appearances.

(2) No trials of any kind to be used.

Step 1
Same as method 1.

Step 2
Add up the two isolated times.

Step 3
Divide by 2 to arrive at an average.

Step 4
Arrange the averaged times in order of speed and then study the form from there.

And that's the third method. It really is very simple, but here are three suggestions for utilising it.

Pay particular attention to this method in high summer, say May–September: Any time-based method will be slightly more reliable in summer when the going at most tracks is consistently good.

Eliminate the dogs with the slowest two averaged times: On the clock, these two dogs will be at a disadvantage to their opponents. How much of a disadvantage will depend on how much slower their times are – so that's always worth a look. Generally speaking though, not many dogs with the two slowest times will go on to win.

If less than .30 of a second separates the slowest and fastest averaged times in the race, think twice about betting on it: With .08 of a second being equivalent to one length, .30 of a second equates to just under four lengths. Not many greyhound races see as little as this between the first and last animals home, but if the method suggests this is going to be the case the contest you are studying is probably going to be a hard one to unravel.

Method 4

This is a method that moves away from using the recent times of each greyhound. Instead, it concentrates on the points table used in Method 1. Again, it is very simple to use.

Step 1
Isolate the three most recent appearances of each greyhound regardless of the distance they were over. Go back no earlier than 42 days.

Step 2
Using the table, and bearing in mind the note underneath it about trials, award points for each of the three isolated appearances.

Step 3
Add the points up and eliminate the dogs with the three lowest scores. Concentrate your form study only on the remaining animals.

Because this method is based solely upon recent finishing positions, the distances of the races contested do not matter. An interesting point about classifying the form in this way is how it will prove much more effective when weighing up higher-grade races. In the better type of contests, previous finishing positions mean more than they do in lower-grade races. Conveniently enough, it is probably the other way around with times.

Notes on this method:

If only one or two points separate the whole field, leave the race alone: As with the other methods, when a narrow band of points exist between the top and bottom rated dogs, winner finding will be hard.

A top-rated dog 3 or more points clear of its opponents will have an outstanding chance: Greyhounds like this will probably be in much better form than their opponents and should be very closely considered.

Consider using forecast bets when two dogs are 3 or more points clear of the rest: In races where this happens, think about backing the two dogs in a forecast bet (to finish first and second). Straight win bets will always be the best way of beating the bookies but races where the top two dogs are at least three points clear of their opponents might be suitable for forecast bets as well.

Method 5

This final method is very different from the other four in as much it neither looks at times nor the vast majority of finishing positions.

Step 1
Search through each race on a card to see if there are any dogs that won by three lengths or more last time out.

Step 2
If any such runners are identified, ensure the greyhound concerned has not been upgraded by more than one level. If they have, they do not qualify.

Step 3

For any greyhounds left, look to see if the phrase MsdTrble (which means missed trouble) exists in the race comments for their win. If it does, the greyhound is not a qualifier.

Step 4

Back any qualifying dogs in each of their next three outings, stopping once they win.

The idea behind this method is to find dogs that have won well enough to suggest they will cope with their upgrade within the next three outings. (Remember, in Great Britain winning greyhounds will only be upgraded at the racing manager's discretion but automatically so in the USA.)

By checking to make sure the dogs were not fortunate to win through missing trouble you will, in effect, be 'validating' the form. Through giving the dog three chances to win in its new grade you will be allowing for bad luck in running. Of course, if the dog returns to its winning grade within those three outings you may well have a real live one on your hands!

There, then, are five methods that can be used either to analyse the form or simply select greyhounds without any further work. Most punters, however, are going to want to do the former and arrive at a selection after exercising their own judgement. In order to do so they need to know how to 'read a race'.

Reading a Race

Reading a race' means knowing what to look for when trying to forecast how the runners will negotiate the course. This is crucial because no matter how good a chance the form of a dog suggests it has, it will not fulfil that promise if it meets trouble in running.

Therefore, let's assume you have used one of the previous methods to select a dog but now you want to know if it will enjoy a reasonably clear run. Alternatively, you may be split between two dogs and want to see which one has the best chance of obtaining a smooth passage.

(Incidentally, if you can't decide between more than two dogs in a race, don't bet. Races where you can't narrow the field down to two or, at the very most three, dogs will probably be too tightly graded to bet serious money on.)

But before we look at how to read a race, it's worth noting that the running style of most greyhounds can be classified under a quite small number of headings. Running style means the way dogs generally run their races. On the whole, greyhounds are remarkably consistent creatures and will normally run their races in broadly the same way time after time.

Fast Starters / Early Pacers

Greyhounds that start their races quickly will generally do so in two ways. Either they will be particularly good at timing the start and will flash out of the traps a length or two in front of the other dogs. Or, they will have lots of early pace. In reality, many fast starting dogs possess both attributes.

However, some dogs do flash out of the traps but are very quickly joined on the run-up (which is the run from the traps to the first bend) by other dogs. These types of animals can be detected through looking at their sectional placing in their previous races. If they are always out of the traps first or second but don't hold their spot at the winning line first time around, they probably lack the sustained early pace necessary to carry them to the first bend in a good position.

Dogs with early pace will emerge from the traps in good positions and at the winning line first time up will still be there – thus maintaining every chance of hitting the first bend in front. The ability to start well and then also show good early pace is an invaluable one. It's something the majority of top class greyhounds are capable of doing.

Middle Pacers

Dogs with middle pace obviously tend to do their fastest running in the middle part of a race. They can be either fast or slow from the traps but, providing they safely negotiate the early bends, will make ground up on the leaders down the back straight. If a greyhound has both decent early and middle pace it will certainly win its fair share of races. Some dogs, however, will show good middle pace but then not last home that strongly. Dogs such as these can often be identified through race comments such as Ld1/2-NrLn.

Slow Starters / Strong Finishers

Lots of greyhounds start their races very slowly and will tend to run the first part of their race right at the back of the field. But from about halfway they will begin to make up ground on the leading dogs. By the time the home straight is reached these big finishers will be close to their full speed and will often come through with spectacularly late runs to snatch a race.

Any greyhounds that are very slowly away will run the first bend right at the back of the field. As a rule, they therefore tend to miss trouble at this vital point. Conversely though, a risk with slow starters is how they will sometimes run straight into the aftermath of collisions or crowding between the front runners. It is certainly not uncommon to see a slow starter badly hampered at the first bend by a greyhound which has been bumped or baulked just a split second earlier.

In keeping with the rest of this chapter, reading a race can be carried out in an organised way through using a number of focal points.

At the Traps

First of all, look at the trap draw for each of the runners. Are there any greyhounds drawn in trap 2 or higher that normally run from trap 1? If there are, it might be that they will attempt to dive onto the rails as soon as the traps open. If you are looking at supporting a dog housed close to the rails this might be something to consider. A dog in any inside trap could have their chances ruined by a runner on its outside diving in front of them right at the start. Previous race comments about dogs having 'railed' will be the thing to look for here.

Just as important, are any wide runners going from traps other than number 6? If there are this could cause trouble for dogs on their outside. If you are considering a dog that is berthed outside of a wide runner, always look at the race comments for the other dog. If there are frequent references to it having run 'very wide' it might cause havoc at the start or at the opening bend. Some dogs used to running from trap 6 will make a dive for the outer part of the track as soon as the traps open.

Also, if your selection is clearly a slow starter, look and see what the animals either side of it normally do at the traps. If one of the dogs next to it also starts slowly there is always a chance a collision will take place as the traps come up. This is because slow starting dogs can sometimes be clumsy as they emerge from the boxes.

Through using the start as the first focal point of a race you will be able to see whether a dog is running the risk of being put out of the contest almost before it has begun. In reality, this does not happen often but it is still a good idea to check!

Winning line first time around

Because almost all racecards give sectional times (the time it took the dogs in their previous races to go from the traps to the winning line first time around) this is an important focal point. Not so much so in races where bends are run before the dogs get there, but certainly in races where the run-up (which is the run from the traps to the first bend) is quite long. Fortunately, in Great Britain and the USA the latter is the case for almost all standard race distances.

It's not hard to work out what to look for with sectional times. If a greyhound has time in hand compared to the dog or dogs either side of it, a trouble free run around the first bend beckons.

Using sectional times, a good way of seeing where a dog might be at the winning line first time up is to simply average out the previous two sets of figures for each runner. Because you will be dealing with only short times – from 2.5 to 4.75 seconds at most British tracks – the differences will not be that great. But they will still be good enough to show if any dog or dogs are likely to flash clear early on in a race.

VICTOR KNIGHT

The First Bend

Probably the point where more races are won or lost than anywhere else. When searching for the winner of a race it is always worthwhile giving a few moments consideration to what might happen at the first bend. When six dogs – eight in the USA – converge at close to top speed around the initial turn anything can happen. That's why greyhounds drawn in traps 1 or 6 frequently hold an advantage. If trouble does occur, the dogs in these traps often slip past it unscathed. So, if you can't decide between two dogs and one of them is housed in either the very inside or the very outside box, think about what might happen at that first bend.

The other thing to note about the first bend is how some dogs just cannot run it cleanly. For whatever reason, a not inconsiderable number of greyhounds never learn how to cope with the hurly burly of the initial corner. It doesn't matter what trap they go from either. They will have little in the way of track-craft (the ability to anticipate and avoid trouble) and will continually find problems.

Dogs like this can be identified through previous race comments such as Blkd1, Bmpd1 or Hmpd1 (which means baulked or bumped or hampered at the first bend). A mistake many greyhound punters make is to keep on thinking dogs like this are unlucky. Instead, they should be considering whether these kinds of dogs are incapable of coming around the first bend unscathed. In other words, they are not unlucky – they simply have no track-craft.

The Second Bend

Not so very long ago, someone produced a set of statistics for one of the top London tracks showing that 70% of the races won there were done so by dogs leading out of the second bend. Perhaps this fact is not as dramatic as it might initially appear though. After all, it's the first bend where most trouble occurs and dogs that race clear out of the second corner may be doing so because they've missed trouble behind them.

So, for the purposes of finding a winner, trying to establish what might happen at the second bend is probably not very important. However, when a race is on always take note of greyhounds that really fly out of

60

the second turn. The second bend is the prelude to the back straight and it's here where good all-round pace really starts to show. Therefore, take note of dogs that impress you with their strength of running out of the second bend. They will probably be in top form.

The Final Bend

Not that much to say about this part of the race, but the little there is should prove valuable when searching for winners. Quite simply, as many dogs cannot race around the first bend without finding trouble, a good few have the same problem on the final bend as well.

This time it's not because they cannot cope with the hurly burly. Instead, it's because they find it difficult to pass another dog without checking up. Therefore, the implication is that the main sufferers of this problem are dogs who win their races through coming with a late run. In practice this is very much the case. Some big-finishing dogs come to the last bend in second or third place travelling considerably stronger than those in front of them. But then a number briefly falter in their stride, undecided whether to pass on the inside or the outside. The hesitation costs them dear as they inevitably choose the wrong route and get baulked or hampered by the runners in front of them. Dogs with good track-craft anticipate where to go at the final bend and win their fair share of races as a result.

Therefore, the message is to avoid dogs with more than a couple of references to Ck4 or Ck6 in their recent race comments. Apart from being clumsy such dogs might be a little unwilling as well. (Ck4 or Ck6 means either checked at the 4th or 6th bend – the final two bends in the majority of races.)

Conclusion

In most races, at least one of these five focal points will prove decisive. So, if you use them as a base for obtaining a picture in your mind's eye of how a race will develop you will be giving yourself a better chance of finding the winner. Even if that isn't the case, a loser might still be avoided because you can't envisage a selection obtaining a clear run. And, in the long term, avoiding losers is just as important as landing winners.

Betting on the Dogs

IT DOESN'T MATTER whether you are a fan in Great Britain, United States of America, Ireland or Australia; greyhound racing is a marvellous sport to bet upon. In the United States and Australia there are only eight or ten runners to choose from and, better still, in Great Britain and Ireland only six. There are many different types of bet as well. Best of all is the straight win bet, but there are also place, show, forecast, Tricast (Trifecta in the States), jackpot and placepot bets available.

This chapter aims to show you how these popular types of bet can be used to make money from greyhound racing. Among other things, the chapter will also show you one way to forecast the price of your selection in a race, methods for using four dogs in trifectas as well as a mention of some greyhound bets to avoid.

Of course, in Great Britain betting can take place either with individual on-course bookmakers, the track tote or in off-course betting shops. In the United States punters do not have as much choice. There are no track bookmakers so dog fans are limited to the Tote. Also, off-track betting is more limited than in Great Britain.

However, there is some compensation in the fact that the amount of money wagered on the Tote in America is much greater than in Great Britain. As a result, winning dividends are often higher. As well as this, because there are eight dogs per race and because Tote turnover is so much greater, dog fans in America have more scope to place multiple bets.

Types of Bet

The Win Bet

First and foremost there is the good old win bet. No matter how attractive the pay-off from any other type of bet appears, punters will inevitably stand the best chance of making money from dog racing through straight win bets. Why? Simply because the profit margin on win bets for both the bookies and the Tote is lower than with any other type of wager.

At every track in either Great Britain, USA, Ireland or Australia, the Tote take-out from the win bet pool is lower than from anything else. For example, at time of writing, Romford Greyhound Stadium in London, was deducting 26% from most of its Tote pools, but only 22% on the one involving win bets. That said, tracks being run by the GRA (Greyhound Racing Authority – the sport's leading promoter) take a 26% deduction from all pools. For most other tracks the deduction from the Tote pools falls between 20% and 25%.

In Great Britain almost all on-course bookies offer win betting only and have to compete with one another while doing so. Therefore, they take chances and will frequently offer slightly better odds than their rivals in an effort to attract more business. For the shrewd punter, this means there are plenty of opportunities to take advantage of. The latter said, however, it is often a very different story in British betting shops. The bookies' profit margins on forecast and Tricast bets are high and the means by which the dividends worked out are very unfavourable to punters. Suffice to say, unless you are playing for fun or with very small stakes, any serious greyhound punter should leave these kind of bets alone.

(In Great Britain, the track dividends for forecast and Tricast bets are not the same as those paid in the shops. The bookies try to reflect the fact that many more people bet on the dogs in the shops than at the tracks. In many ways this is understandable but the methods now used to calculate forecast and Tricast dividends allow the bookies plenty of room for error – and that's putting it politely.)

When placing a win bet with the on-course bookmakers, a punter needs to simply name their selection (usually by trap number) along with the amount of money they want on it, e.g. £10 win trap 4. At the same time they hand over the cash and receive a numbered ticket in return.

Newcomers to this form of betting are often confused by how the ticket they receive has no information on it concerning the wager. But they need not worry. The bookmaker's clerk will have recorded the number of the ticket in his ledger. In this ledger, the clerk will record every bet on the race. From this they will be able to calculate how much the bookmaker stands to win or lose on a race no matter what the result. It follows, therefore, that it is the clerk's duty to be accurate in his or her work. Indeed, given the amount of on-course bets that are stuck, the number of disputes between bookies and punters is amazingly low.

There are three secrets to making a profit from straight win betting on the dogs.

(1) Pick the right dogs! Hopefully the preceding chapters will have pointed you in the right direction here.

(2) Try to obtain the best odds, making sure they offer value as well. We'll examine this in just a moment.

(3) Operate a money-management betting system. This is something that applies equally well to whatever types of bet are being placed. In the next chapter, we'll look at money-management for greyhound race betting in a bit more detail. But first, let's return to point number 2.

Obtaining the best odds might seem like common sense but although many punters appreciate it's the thing to do, relatively few know how to go about it. Unfortunately, value is something that is now widely misunderstood by many punters. Of course, much of what follows will apply only to Great Britain but value is value wherever you are betting and the principles will hold true anywhere in the world.

There are a number of things that need to be done in order to obtain the best odds. Firstly, punters will need to obtain knowledge of how on-course bookies calculate their prices. Secondly, they will have to develop a method for predicting the price of their selection. Thirdly, once at the track, they will have to keep their eyes open and their wits about them ready to dive in take the best prices.

First, let's see how bookies form their prices. In other words, how they operate.

In Great Britain, the majority of dog races are made up of six runners. Let's imagine that such a race sees each runner with an equal chance. In theory then, the odds on each dog should be 5/1. For the bookmaker, however, this would be no good at all. It's unlikely each dog would be supported with the same amount of money, but if they were the bookie would only be paying out exactly what he had taken in. In reality it's far more likely that each of the dogs would be supported with different amounts of cash. But that would be no good for the bookies either because, depending on which dog won the race, they would either win a lot or lose a lot. So, what do they do?

The answer is to try to build a profit margin into the race through the use of their prices. Again using our race where each runner has a completely equal chance, instead of offering 5/1 on every dog the bookie would probably offer 4/1 or 9/2. Thus, if an equal amount of money was taken on every runner the bookie would end up paying out less than they took in no matter which greyhound came first.

On paper it looks like this. Each runner has a perfectly equal chance of winning so, in theory, should be 5/1. Let's assume the bookie takes £100 on each dog. In total, they will take £600 but as you can see from the liability on each runner, they will make a profit of £100 no matter which dog wins the race.

Trap 1	–	Twilight Time	-	odds 4/1	- liability	£500
				(400 won, plus return of £100 stake)		
Trap 2	–	Bookworm	-	odds 4/1	- liability	£500	ditto
Trap 3	–	Mystery Girl	-	odds 4/1	- liability	£500	ditto
Trap 4	–	Top of the Hill	-	odds 4/1	- liability	£500	ditto
Trap 5	–	Camelot	-	odds 4/1	- liability	£500	ditto
Trap 6	–	Hot Shoes	-	odds 4/1	- liability	£500	ditto

(Of course, on most occasions bookmakers will not take an equal amount of money for each runner. But they can overcome this in a number of ways. Firstly, they can lay bets off with other bookies and thus reduce their liabilities. Secondly, they can adjust their prices to try to balance things up. Lastly, they may not try to achieve a balanced book to start with. Instead, they might offer better prices than their rivals on just one or two dogs in the race so as to reflect their own opinion about what they feel can and cannot win. In fact, this third option is by far and away the most commonly used one.)

However, for the moment let's stick to the theory. In our example the bookie would make a £100 profit no matter which dog won the race. Using an age-old betting term, the book would be over-round.

What punters need to do in order to obtain the best prices – and to also spot value – is know the way to work out whether a book is over-round. By far the best way of doing this is to convert the prices into percentages as shown in the table on the next page and then add the percentages up. When the final figure is greater than 100% a bookmaker is said to have an over-round book. When it is less than 100% it is said to be over-broke. The good news with over-broke books is that every runner in a race could be backed and a profit shown no matter what the result. Needless to say, over-broke books don't happen very often.

NB: when an over-round figure is fairly low (say between 105% and 112%) the prices are not likely to increase. But when a bookmaker has an over-round figure of 125% or more, their prices will almost certainly be extended. Generally speaking, bookmakers open up the betting with highly over-round books but, as the race nears, they will extend their prices. Calculating over-round and over-broke figures is particularly relevant for greyhound race punters. This is because with only six runners in the majority of races the calculations will not take long.

ODDS AS PERCENTAGES TABLE

Odds	Percentage	Odds	Percentage
2 / 5	71.40%	3 / 1	25.00%
4 / 9	69.20%	100 / 30	23.10%
1 / 2	66.66%	7 / 2	22.20%
8 / 15	65.20%	4 / 1	20.00%
4 / 7	63.60%	9 / 2	18.20%
8 / 13	61.90%	5 / 1	16.67%
4 / 6	60.00%	11 / 2	15.40%
8 / 11	57.90%	6 / 1	14.30%
4 / 5	55.55%	13 / 2	13.40%
10 / 11	52.30%	7 / 1	12.50%
Evens	50.00%	5 / 2	11.80%
11 / 10	47.60%	8 / 1	11.10%
5 / 4	44.40%	10 / 1	9.10%
11 / 8	42.10%	12 / 1	7.70%
6 / 4	40.00%	14 / 1	6.66%
13 / 8	38.10%	16 / 1	5.88%
7 / 4	36.40%	20 / 1	4.76%
15 / 8	34.80%	25 / 1	3.85%
2 / 1	33.33%	33 / 1	2.94%
9 / 4	30.70%	50 / 1	1.96%
5 / 2	28.70%	100 / 1	0.99%
11 / 4	26.70%	200 / 1	0.50%

Having seen how a bookie tries to operate, remember, in practice, they are frequently unable to do so because not enough money will be taken on every runner. Instead, they frequently try to take more money on just one or two runners in the hope they will not win. As far as punters are concerned though, this makes no difference to the way odds should be converted into percentages.

Place and Show Bets

As an alternative to win bets, punters in Great Britain can back dogs for a place but, unfortunately, only at the track. In the United States they can support a greyhound to either place or show. For a place bet in both countries to be successful, the dog supported must finish first or second. In the States, a show bet pays out when the greyhound finishes first, second or third – this being made possible because of the eight runner races. The thing to remember about both these bets is that the money wagered goes into individual pools along with all the other bets of the same type.

Sadly, in Great Britain apart from busy nights at the major tracks, place betting is not worth considering as a serious betting medium. The amount of money attracted into the place pools is minimal and the resultant dividends generally poor. The situation is slightly better in the United States but at the smaller tracks the same problem tends to exist as in Great Britain.

So poor is the place betting situation in Great Britain, there is nothing of any real use that can be said about it. For the States, however, there are a couple of tips to bear in mind.

Never support a greyhound for a place that is showing on the win pool to be even money or shorter. In fact, with dogs like this it is probably better to support them with a show bet rather than a place. Generally speaking, the show dividend on such short-priced dogs will be much the same as for the place one but you will have an extra chance of collecting. Of course, though, supporting even money or worse shots for a place or a show is not the best way to win money from greyhound racing!

Place bets in the United States/Australia are best used when a dog is 5/1 or greater on the win pool but, nevertheless, appears to have a good chance of making the frame. Races where the favourite is fairly short – say 2/1 to 11/4 – often throw up a second or third favourite about the 5/1 mark. It is these dogs that can make for decent place bets.

As we've just discussed, show bets are only available in the United States and Australia. There is one strategy for using them that can be quite effective. It involves looking for races where there is a strong favourite as well as a longer shot that you feel has a good chance of winning. The idea is to support the longer shot to win and the favourite to show. If the longer shot wins you'll enjoy a nice pay-off. If it doesn't, you'll still have a good chance of your stake being returned through the show bet on the favourite paying out. The theory being a short priced favourite should have every chance of reaching the first three places. There is also the golden scenario where the long-shot wins and the favourite finishes second or third, thus making both of your bets winning ones!

Jackpot and Placepot Bets

In Great Britain, punters can place Jackpot or Placepot bets. Jackpot bets involve trying to find up to seven or eight winners with the stake for the bet going into a specific Tote pool and are only available at the tracks. Anyone smart enough to find the winners takes a share of this pool. Needless to say, this is easier said then done. Because of this not all tracks operate the jackpot bet but those that do sometimes see the pool build up to a sizeable amount.

There is only one serious way that the jackpot can be tackled and that's through picking more than one dog in each of the nominated races – in other words, through a permutation bet. It's not a bet to be taken too seriously unless the pool at a track you visit has become very high. Then it might be time to step in and have a go. If you are going to chase a jackpot, an easy way of working out how many permutations you will need to cover is through multiplying together the number of selections you are making in each race.

So, let's suppose the jackpot at your track covers six races. You have selected greyhounds in each of these races as follows:

Race 1 =	2 dogs	
Race 2 =	3 dogs	
Race 3 =	1 dog (your banker)	
Race 4 =	2 dogs	
Race 5 =	3 dogs	
Race 6 =	2 dogs	

If you multiply 2 x 3 x 1 x 2 x 3 x 2 you arrive at 72. Thus, cover for 72 bets would be required. Note how race 3 has only a single selection. For most punters, putting in one or two bankers will be essential otherwise the cost of 'perming' becomes too high.

Placepot bets are much the same but with two important differences. Firstly, it is not the tracks that offer this kind of bet but the betting shops. On most afternoon greyhound meetings a bet called the 'Placer' will be available. A 'placer' involves trying to find a dog to finish first or second in either the first or last six races of a 12 race card. Again, permutations are the answer but it is worth noting how the betting shop chains have agreed a formula for working out the dividends on successful 'placer' wagers. Needless to say, again it's a formula that ensures the betting shops do OK from this type of bet.

Forecast and Tricast Bets

As either an alternative or an addition to win, place and show bets, punters can also place forecasts or Tricasts. Although still very popular in Great Britain, Tricasts (or Trifectas as they are known in the United States) tend to be the staple diet of American greyhound racing fans. Forecast bets, probably more heavily played in Great Britain than in America, involve trying to predict the first two greyhounds home. Tricasts, more heavily played in the USA, involve trying to find the first three past the post.

In Great Britain, one of the most popular forecasts is the three-dog combination. Here, punters pick three greyhounds and cover all the combinations of two, of which there are six. An example makes this clear.

Traps 1 – 5 – 6 selected.

Six combinations possible.

| 1 – 5 | 5 – 6 | 6 – 1 |
| 1 – 6 | 5 – 1 | 6 – 5 |

Thus, if any two of the dogs in traps 1, 5 or 6 finish first and second in either order the forecast will be landed. For an outlay of six units, this type of bet can be quite useful – providing the three dogs selected are not the first three in the betting. If they are, the dividend on any successful forecast will be low and may well fail to cover the initial stake.

A good way of utilising this bet is to select the favourite alongside the fourth and fifth in the betting. If the fourth or fifth in the betting wins with the favourite second, the dividend can be quite a tidy one. Even if the favourite wins, beating into second one of the other two selections, the dividend, although smaller, might be quite good as well.

An alternative way of forecast betting – and something a number of professional punters do – is to support one dog to win with the bookies but also put it in a forecast to come second to the third or fourth in the betting. Through doing this you'll be putting in place a limited, but inexpensive, form of cover on your win bet.

In the United Sates, over 50% of all the money bet at any dog track is on the Trifecta. Although not so popular in Great Britain, Tricasts still form a considerable amount of a track's Tote betting turnover. The reason, however, Trifecta bets are so popular in the United States is because of the eight dog races. With eight dogs, there are 336 possible combinations of three but with 6 runners there are only 120. Thus, trifecta dividends are higher in America simply because more money goes into the pool and it is divided more ways.

Trifecta strategy always forms a large part of any American greyhound betting book. We won't go into this topic in as much detail but we will consider a couple of ideas that derive from the United States. Before that though, let's consider an idea or two for tricast betting on Great Britain's six dog contests.

The key to successful tricast betting is to place combination bets. Any punter who bases a tricast strategy around a single combination of dogs is not going to win often enough to make this form of betting pay. On the other hand, any punter who covers too many combinations is going to fail as well.

The happiest medium is to put no more than four dogs in any one bet. The following table shows you how many possible combinations of three (remember, you are trying to predict the first three home) there are in six, five, four and three dogs.

Number of Dogs	Total Number of Combinations
3	6
4	24
5	60
6	120

So, if you select, say, five dogs and want to cover every possible tricast combination it will cost you 60 times whatever your unit stake is. In the vast majority of cases this will be too much because the dividends on British tracks will rarely be high enough to cover this kind of outlay. No, five-dog coverage is too much but four is a different matter. Through using four dogs as the basis for Tricast betting you will increase your chances of making a long-term profit.

One way of using four dogs is through simply covering every possible combination of three within them. That will mean an outlay of 24 bets. In some cases this will be fine, providing the four dogs do not contain the favourite. However, punters often find it difficult to leave the favourite out of a four dog combination because they cannot envisage the market leader failing to finish in the first three.

So, the first idea for Tricast betting is to look for races where you are convinced a short-priced favourite – say one at 2/1 or worse – cannot win. Then, put four of the other dogs in a tricast bet and cover every possible combination, a total of 24 bets. If one of these combinations comes up you'll find the dividend will probably be good enough to give you a fair profit. The theory here is that if a really short favourite is not going to win it will be down to trouble in running. Thus it won't even finish in the first three.

However, an even better way of using four dogs in a tricast bet is as follows. Look at each of the four dogs and decide upon one or two that you feel cannot win the race. Then, place a Tricast bet excluding the combinations that include those dogs finishing first. For every dog you do not nominate to win, the bet is reduced by six combinations. For example, if your four dogs are housed in traps 1,2,3 and 4 and you want full Tricast cover it will cost you 24 bets. But if you decide trap 4 cannot win, the bet will involve an outlay of 18 bets. If you decide traps 3 and 4 cannot win, the bet will only involve cover for 12 combinations.

This idea reduces the cost of covering four dogs in a tricast and can lead to some useful payoffs. Of course, limiting the number of combinations need not be restricted to eliminating dogs you feel cannot win. You could equally well pick a dog (or dogs) and miss the combination out that has them finishing second or third. That said, trying to predict a dog will not finish second might be a little difficult – remember, you'll still be forecasting it to win or come third – but predicting a dog not to finish third is more practical. This strategy might be useful in races where there is a strong favourite. Saying that you think such a greyhound must finish first or second might make good sense in tricast combination bets.

As regards Trifecta bets in the United States, here's a table showing you how many possible combinations of three there are in eight dog races.

Number of Dogs	Total Number of Combinations
3	6
4	24
5	60
6	120
7	210
8	336

As we saw earlier, there are a large number of combinations available with eight dogs. Hence, the popularity of this type of bet in the United States. One of the most commonly used trifecta bets in America is the limited wheel. The idea is to give yourself as much coverage as possible for the least amount of cost.

A limited wheel bet involves finding a 'key' dog. This key dog will have to finish first or second for bets of this type to come up. A limited wheel also involves eliminating as many as of the other runners as possible.

Let's look at an example.

Supposing you have eliminated three dogs from a race (traps 2, 6 and 7). Also, you have landed on the dog in trap 5 as your key runner.

Key Dog	Trap 5	(Win)
Four Dangers	Traps 1, 3, 4, 8	(Place)
	Traps 1, 3, 4, 8	(Show)

This gives 12 possible combinations. Trap 5 must win the race but any two of the dogs in traps 1, 3, 4 or 8 can finish second and third in any order for the bet to be successful.

Alternatively, you could wheel trap 5 into both first and second position. This bet would be laid out as follows.

Key Dog	Trap 5 (Win)		1,3,4,8 (Win)
Four Dangers	Traps 1,3,4,8 (Place)	+	5 (Place)
	Traps 1,3,4,8 (Show)		1,3,4,8 (Show)

So, trap 5 can now finish first or second. Any of the dogs in traps 1,3,4 and 8 can finish in the other two positions in any order. There are 24 combinations in this bet.

Note: Many studies in the United States have shown it is not worth extending the bet to put the key dog into the show position. The figures demonstrate how key dogs don't run into third spot often enough to justify the cost of putting them in this position within Trifecta bets. It's a valid point. Dogs with good enough form to be thought of as key runners should be able to finish in the first two. If they don't it's probably going to be down to a rough passage in running. If that's the case they will probably finish nearer the back of the field than the front.

Greyhound Forecast Multiple Betting

Here is a chart showing the number of forecast double and treble bets required (for use in betting shops in Great Britain).

GREYHOUND FORECAST BETTING

No. Races	Straight Forecast Doubles	Reverse Forecast Doubles	2 Pairs Rev. F/C Doubles	3 Dogs Rev. F/C Doubles	Straight Forecast Trebles	Reverse Forecast Trebles	2 Pairs Rev. F/C Trebles	3 Dogs Rev. F/C Trebles
2	1	4	16	36	–	–	–	–
3	3	12	48	108	1	8	64	216
4	6	24	96	216	4	32	256	864
5	10	40	160	360	10	80	640	2160
6	15	60	240	540	20	160	1280	4320
7	21	84	336	756	35	280	2240	7560
8	28	112	448	1008	56	448	3584	12096
9	36	144	576	1296	84	672	5376	18144
10	45	180	720	1620	120	960	7680	25920
11	55	220	880	1980	165	1320	10560	35640
12	66	264	1056	2376	220	1760	14080	47520
13	78	312	1248	2808	286	2288	18304	61776
14	91	364	1456	3276	364	2912	23296	78624

Value and pricing up a selection

Before we move on to look at one way punters can try to predict the price of their selection, let's first briefly discuss value.

Nowadays, punters constantly hear about the need to obtain value when they bet. Trouble is, it has become an over-used word. As a result many punters now have a mistaken belief about what value is. No matter what is being bet upon, value can be defined as follows: If the true odds of an event occurring are less than the betting odds that can be obtained about that event, good value must therefore exist. Spinning a coin is the best example.

There are only two possible outcomes to the spinning of a coin. It can either come down heads or tails. So, the true odds of calling the correct result is 50%, 1 to 1, or evens as it is better known. Therefore, if you bet £1 at evens on heads over a series of 10,000 spins you should lose £1 half the time but win £1 the other half – thus you'd neither win nor lose. (Here it should be pointed out that there is no guarantee 10,000 spins would produce 5,000 heads and 5,000 tails. However, the law of averages suggests it would be a close run thing and the higher the number of spins the tighter it would be thanks to something called standard deviation. Also, in the absence of anything else, the law of average is the best thing to use when discussing matters such as this.)

But if, before the series of spins started, a bookie decided to offer you 6/4 on calling the correct result each time, value would be staring you in the face. All you would need to do is make the same call every spin and, in theory, you must win.

Every time the coin came down the wrong way you'd lose your £1. But every time it went your way you'd get back £2.50 from betting £1 at 6/4. So, over the whole series you'd expect to lose £5,000 but receive back £12,500 (5,000 x £2.50). At the end of the series you'd therefore make a profit of £2,500 (i.e. £10,000 staked and £12,500 returned).

Nice work, but gambling on sports – dog racing just as much as anything else – is not as simple as that. This is because the true odds cannot be so easily defined. The odds on greyhound racing, the same as with horse racing, are a matter of opinion. So, the question of value is subjective. However, what many punters fail to appreciate is that value can exist in short prices as well as in long ones.

In dog racing, the trick when looking for value is to balance up the chances of each dog winning against the price about it doing so. It might be that a 6/4 shot looks to have an evens chance of winning. Most punters, though, would never consider a 6/4 shot to be value. In most cases they would be right but the point is, because value is subjective, it can exist even in short prices.

Taking value a step further, real professional dog punters sometimes don't back the runner with the most obvious chance of winning. Instead, they back the dog that they consider to have a better chance than their price suggests. i.e. a dog that is 6/4 might look to have a clear-cut chance of landing the spoils – 6/4 being a reflection of that chance. But a dog with not such obvious credentials could be 4/1 when it might actually have a 3/1 chance of winning. Professional punters would probably back the 4/1 shot because the value they are obtaining compensates for the fact the dog's chances are not as good as the one at 6/4. Over a period of time, they know there is more chance of making a profit betting in this way than through sticking to the obvious.

That said, don't make looking for dogs with longer prices your primary aim. Always consider the form first and then weigh up the chances of each dog against the prices on offer. Through doing so you'll soon get the hang of knowing when value exists.

Pricing a dog yourself

Trying to predict what the price of your selection is going to be will stand you in very good stead once you start backing greyhounds on a serious basis. Above all, you'll know when the bookies are offering a value price.

However, working out the price you think your selection should be is not as straightforward as it might seem. Not many people bother to do it, but those that do – the bookies and a handful of professionals – tend to price up the whole field.

What follows, though, is a method for predicting the price of an individual greyhound. This will be quicker than pricing up a whole field and, after all, it's the price of your selection that's the most relevant thing. Furthermore, if you use the table given previously to work out what percentage over-round (or over-broke) the bookmakers are betting to, you'll know what way the prices are most likely to move anyway.

Note: This is an important point. If you work out your selection should be 3/1 and, once betting begins, it quickly settles at that price you'll know you were not too far wrong. However, if the percentage figure for the whole book is very high you'll also know it will probably be the prices on some of the other dogs that will increase rather than the one on yours.

There are a number of ways to price up one or more dogs in a race but the following method is as good as any and, although it might appear a little involved, it doesn't take long to learn.

To make it easier, let's break the method down into a series of quick steps.

(1) Start off by putting a price of 5/1 down for your selection. The idea here is to assume your selection has as much chance of winning as its opponents in the race.

(2) Look at each of the other greyhounds in turn and, bearing in mind whatever selection method you used, assess what danger to your selection you feel each of the other dogs are.

(3) Rate the threat of each of the other dogs on a scale of 0, ½ or 1 point. So, every dog you were completely able to dismiss would be awarded 1 point. But, if your analysis of a race had left you thinking it lay between just two dogs, the one of these you didn't pick would be awarded zero. (Initially, this might seem strange but stick with it because everything will become clear in a moment.) A dog falling somewhere between the two – it might have a great trap draw but fairly modest recent form – would be awarded half a point. (You'll get the hang of it once you've tried it a few times!)

(4) Assess the other threats to your selection winning the race. Perhaps your dog has a bad trap draw and you feel this considerably reduces its chance of winning – if this was the case you'd rate it a 0 point factor.

(5) Once the threat of each dog, plus any other factors, have been quantified into points, simply take the points total away from five. The figure you are left with is the provisional price for your selection (it is also your view of what its true price should be). However, one more step remains.

(6) Take the figure you arrived at in step 5 and reduce it by 17.5%. This figure is a general assumption of the profit figure the bookies aim to make on a race. You'll need to adjust this so as to take into account of how the bookies operate at whatever track you are betting at. At this point, do remember you are trying to predict what price your selection will be at the track. Hence, the bookie's profit margin must be taken into account.

The idea behind this method is as follows: You start off by assuming your selection has a 5/1 chance of winning the race because, numerically speaking, there are five other dogs that can beat it. You then reduce this by taking away each half or full point awarded to the dogs seen as being either a partial or non-existent threat to yours. Obviously, a dog seen as a zero point danger would mean the price of your selection not being reduced. Equally so, if the trap draw of your selection looks difficult you would want to have that reflected in the odds.

It may seem odd awarding zero points to full-blown threats to your selection but the more opponents your dog has to beat the longer its price should be. Also, the more potentially adverse factors your dog looks like it will have to overcome should make the price longer. Remember, the idea is to arrive at a price for your selection winning the race. Anything that is not seen as a danger to that happening will reduce the odds and vice-versa.

In practice this method might look like this.

Trap 1	-	Sunshine Boy	0 point threat.
Trap 2	-	Autumn Sunset	½ point threat
Trap 3	-	Winter's Tale	1 point threat.
Trap 4	-	Spring to It	1 point threat.
Trap 5	-	Four Seasons	½ point threat
Trap 6	-	All the Year (Your selection)	N/A
Other factors			0 point threat.

This would mean a total of 3 points being deducted from the 5/1. Thus, following your analysis, your selection has a 2/1 chance of winning. But the bookies' profit must be allowed for. In theory at least, this profit comes from the prices being adjusted downwards, so the 2/1 needs one final sum performed upon it.

Assuming a profit margin of 17.5%, adjust the 2/1 as follows.

> 2/1 multiplied by 17.5% is 0.35.
> 2/1 minus 0.35 is 1.65.

Adjust that figure to the nearest set of odds used and you arrive at 13/8 (1.625/1).

So, the analysis ends with you believing your dog should be around the 13/8 mark.

All of this will probably seem very complicated to begin with but don't allow that to put you off. Once you are used to it this method will surprise you with its accuracy. Obviously, its success will depend on your skill at assessing the threat of the other dogs but with practice you'll soon get a feel for this. There is one final thing to note though.

Once you've become skilled with this method you'll be genuinely surprised how useful it is. But never allow it to 'bog' you down. In other words, if you assess a dog to have a 3/1 chance and it never moves beyond 5/2 or 11/4, don't refrain from backing it! You must allow for some misjudgement on your own part. To miss a winner because of a ¼ point difference would be foolish. Perhaps the best suggestion is to allow up to ½ a point either way. Again, you'll soon get the feel for this kind of thing.

Major US Totalisator bets.

Win, Place or Show: If you bet on a dog to win, you only collect if your selection comes in first. With a place bet you collect if your selection comes first or second. You collect on a show bet if your dog comes first, second or third. Obviously, the payoff for win bets is greater than for place bets and greater for place best than for show bets.

Daily Double: Involves picking the winners of the first and second races in a bet that, naturally, has to be placed before the first race.

Quinella: Correctly pick the two dogs, in any order, in the same race to collect.

Quinella Double: Involves picking the first and second dogs, in any order, in the last two races of each meeting.

Perfecta: Picking the first two greyhounds home, in exact order, in any race.

Trifecta: Selecting the first three greyhounds home in a single race. The first of the bets on USA tracks that can pay really big money.

Superfecta: Same as Trifecta, but the first four dogs home – spectacular payoffs!

Bet Three: Involves selecting the winners of three consecutive races. Bet must be placed before the start of the first Bet Three race (the Bet Three races are nominated by individual track operators.)

Other bets: Individual tracks offer jackpot style bets (finding the winner of a whole series of races for sometimes huge payoffs, as well as bets like the "Twin Trifecta" where the first three home have to be found in a nominated race. If successful, punters then exchange their tickets for a payoff plus a chance to again predict the first three home in a later race.

Money-Management

NO MATTER WHAT type of bet is employed, without a money management system (also known as a staking plan) a punter will have little chance of making long-term profits from any kind of gambling. This is particularly the case with greyhound racing because there are so many races on a card. So, wherever in the world you do your dog punting, the following methods for managing your betting cash should prove invaluable.

Before looking at them, though, do note that these are methods based upon a fairly cautious approach to punting. Also, some of the strike rates quoted may seem hard to achieve but achievable they are with good judgement and the discipline to stop betting at the right time.

Method 1

This initial method is the simplest one of all and is based upon two things. Firstly, how many winners you can reasonably expect to find and, secondly, the amounts of money you bet in.

No matter how long they have been in the profession, even the very best newspaper tipsters – dogs or horses – rarely achieve a long-term strike rate of better than 30-35%. That's to say, over a whole year the best a tipster might hope to do is find three winners out of every ten selections. Short-term, they might do better or they might do worse but a 30% strike-rate will keep them in their jobs. (Some punters may think this is still a high strike rate but look at the naps table for horse racing tipsters. You'll see that the top ten or so of them do generally manage to maintain a 30% strike rate.)

Therefore, this first money-management method is based upon not trying to better a 30% strike rate. For example, at a meeting where a punter intends to bet in six races – whatever the type of bets – they should consider stopping when, or if, two of the bets are successful. The reasoning here being how two winners out of six bets achieves a 33%

strike rate. OK, the six bets will not all be struck but the law of averages suggest that if they were no further winners would be found.

Of course, some common sense needs to be applied. If a punter finds the first two bets out of an intended six are successful they should seriously consider going home with profit intact. However, if a second winner is found with the fifth of six bets it might be sensible to carry on and support the last selection as well. The principle behind this method is to respect long established trends and go along with them in order to protect profits.

Many argue this idea is flawed because there will be days when all bets will be unsuccessful. Remember though, on days like these you will be no worse off using this idea than you would through backing all of your selections with any other method. Another argument put forward against this idea is how there will be days when the 30% strike-rate could be bettered but won't be because you will have stopped betting. This is a fair point but let's consider something experienced punters often notice.

They often comment on how, at the end of a series of bets that began with a winner, they finish up the same amount of money in front as they were after that first success. It is very rare to find a winner with every bet and any punter believing this will happen is not going to last long backing greyhounds! Surely it is far better to be realistic and try and protect profits won early on than give them back in the vain hope all your selections are going to win? Not everyone will agree but it's worth considering.

The second part of this method depends on the amounts of money you bet in. Quite simply, all you do is decide upon an amount of money that you would be satisfied with winning at a meeting. Then, whenever you reach that amount, stop betting. Obviously, the amount of money you stop at will be dependent on the size of your stakes. Again, the principle behind this method is to retain profits rather than keep chasing winners and, more often than not, give the money back.

Method 2

The next idea is for use with a series of three bets. Employing it by only having three bets a meeting would be ideal but not essential. So, for example, if six selections were made for one meeting the method would be used twice. Its rules are as follows:

- 1 point on the opening selection.
- If a selection loses, double the stake on the next bet.
- If a selection wins, stake half the profit on the next bet (remember, each point can be for whatever unit stake you wish).

It's a very simple staking plan originally designed to operate as a separate entity for each meeting. Let's take a look at it in action with three examples, comparing it each time to a level stakes plan (level stakes are where the same amount is staked on every bet).

Stake	1 point	1 point	2 points
Result	W2/1	L	L
Profit or Loss	+ 2 points	-1 point	-1 point
Overall Outcome = Loss of 1 point			
(Using level stakes, the outcome would have been = Break Even)			

Stake	1 point	2 points	4 points
Result	L	L	W2/1
Profit or Loss	-1 point	-3 points	+5 points
Overall Outcome = Profit of 5 points.			
(Using level stakes, the outcome would have been = Break Even)			

Stake	1 point	1 point	2 points
Result	W2/1	L	W3/1
Profit or Loss	+2 points	+1 point	+ 7 points
Overall Outcome = Profit of 7 points.			
(Using level stakes, the outcome would have been = + 4 points)			

Of course, the outcome of using this staking method will always depend on the amount of winners found, the price of those winners and the pattern they occur in. But, generally speaking, it will prove more effective than betting at level stakes. Incidentally, any plans that involve doubling up after a loser are normally best avoided. This one, however, is based upon a three bet sequence only and thus a punter using it can never lose more than 7 times their unit stake.

Method 3

This third method is ideal for meetings where four to twelve selections have been made. Stakes are again increased after losers but only on a very conservative basis.

Its rules are as follows:

- Stakes to be on the progression of 1 point, 1 point, 2 points, 3 points.
- After a winner, revert to 1 point.
- After four consecutive losers, revert to 1 point.

Let's look at a couple of examples, again compared to level stakes.

Stake	1pt	1pt	1pt	2pts	3pts	1pt	1pt	1pt	1pt	1pt
Result	W2/1	L	L	L	W2/1	W3/1	L	W2/1	L	L
Profit or Loss	+2pts	+1pt	-	-2pts	+4pts	+7pts	+6pts	+7pts	+6pts	+5pts

Overall Outcome = Profit of 5 points.

(Using level stakes, the outcome would have been = Profit of 3 points)

Stake	1pt	1pt	1pt	2pts	3pts	1pt	1pt	1pt	2pts	3pts
Result	W2/1	L	L	L	L	W2/1	L	L	L	W3/1
Profit or Loss	+2pts	+1pt	-	-2pts	-5pts	-3pts	-4pts	-5pts	-7pts	+2pts

Overall Outcome = Profit of 2 points

(Using level stakes, the outcome would have been = Break Even)

Naturally, all staking plan examples can always be manipulated to show them in a favourable light. However, the staking ideas we have looked at so far will be of assistance to greyhound punters providing, of course, they are used on a consistent basis.

At this point, it must be noted that all the money management ideas in this chapter, the first two have been no exception, are designed for working with straight win bets. Anyone who uses forecasts as their primary weapon in the battle against the bookies will struggle to find a staking plan that is of any use. This is because forecast dividends are so erratic. Also, forecasts are much harder to land and so the win-frequency will be significantly less.

Method 4

So far, we have looked at money management plans that are based around one meeting. But now we are going to consider a method that can be run on a meeting to meeting basis and then halted after a period of time – or amount of profit – chosen by the operator.

Before we do this, let's first dispel the myth about a commonly used staking plan. A plan similar in concept to the one we will be looking at but which is definitely not as punter-friendly. It involves betting a predetermined percentage of a pre-set bank. Its rules are as follows:

- Set a bank to bet with.
- Decide on an initial amount of stake.
- Calculate what percentage of the bank the initial stake is.
- Bet that percentage figure no matter how the bank total fluctuates.
- Set a new bank when, or if, a certain amount of profit is reached on the original one.

Let's see this idea in action with the following example.

- £1000 bank decided upon.
- £100 initial amount of stake.
- Thus, 10% is percentage figure.
- No matter how bank fluctuates, 10% will always be amount bet.
- Set a new bank when original one has grown to £2,000.

So, in practice across a series of seven bets this is what would happen.

Bet No 1:	£100 win at 5/1	W5/1	Bank £1,500
Bet No 2:	£150 win at 6/4	L6/4	Bank £1,350
Bet No 3:	£135 win at 2/1	L2/1	Bank £1,215
Bet No 4:	£121 win at 2/1	W2/1	Bank £1,457
Bet No 5:	£145 win at 1/1	L1/1	Bank £1,312
Bet No 6:	£131 win at 2/1	L2/1	Bank £1,181
Bet No 7:	£118 win at 6/4	W6/4	Bank £1,358
Outlay: £900	Profit: £358		

Even with this series of seven bets showing an extremely difficult to achieve 43% strike-rate, any punter using this plan would have been almost £100 worse off compared to betting with £100 level stakes. Sticking to £100 stakes would have yielded a profit of £450 for an outlay of only £700.

This is a good example of how betting a percentage of the bank is probably not the way forward for punters. Only when a number of winners are found in very close succession is betting in this way preferable to using level stakes. Admittedly, winners do often come in batches but certainly not always tightly enough to justify using a percentage staking system. Instead, why not consider employing this one.

Rules:

- Set a bank of, say, 100 points.
- Divide the bank into units to arrive at the initial stake.
- Profits from each winning bet are to be added to the bank and losses deducted.
- Stakes never to fall below whatever they were originally set at regardless of the amount in the bank.

With this system, the final rule is essential. It means that when the bank goes above its starting point stakes will be increased. They will then remain at their new level even if the bank falls back again – and even if it dips beneath its starting point.

Let's look at this method in practice.

- Bank set at 100 points with £10 per point (£1000 bank)
- Divide bank by 20 units to arrive at an initial stake of £50

Results as follows:

STAKE	RESULT	PROFIT	LOSS	BANK
				£1000.00
£50.00	Won2/1	£100.00		£1100.00
£55.00	Lost		£55.00	£1045.00
£55.00	Lost		£55.00	£990.00
£55.00	Lost		£55.00	£935.00
£55.00	Lost		£55.00	£880.00
£55.00	Won5/1	£275.00		£1155.00
£58.00	Lost			£1097.00
£58.00	Won4/1	£232.00		£1329.00
£66.00	Lost		£66.00	£1263.00
£66.00	Lost		£66.00	£1197.00
£66.00	Won2/1	£132.00		£1329.00
£66.00	Lost		£66.00	£1263.00
£66.00	Won5/2	£165.00		£1428.00
£71.00	Lost		£71.00	£1357.00
£71.00	Won6/4	£106.50		£1463.50
£73.00	Lost		£73.00	£1390.50
£73.00	Lost		£73.00	£1317.50
£73.00	Lost		£73.00	£1244.50
£73.00	Lost		£73.00	£1171.50
£73.00	Won5/2	£182.50		£1354.00
£73.00	Won4/1	£292.00		£1646.00
£82.00	Won6/4	£123.00		£1769.00
£88.00	Lost		£88.00	£1681.00
£88.00	Lost		£88.00	£1593.00
£88.00	Won4/1	£332.00		£1945.00
£97.00	Lost		£97.00	£1848.00
£97.00	Lost		£97.00	£1751.00
£97.00	Lost		£97.00	£1654.00
£97.00	Won3/1	£291.00		£1945.00
£97.00	Lost		£97.00	£1848.00
£97.00	Lost		£100.00	£1748.00

Over this series of 31 bets the profit on the 11 winners comes to £1,748.00. Admittedly, that's a high strike-rate of about 35% but if the stakes had remained at a level £50 the profit would have been £1,600. So, on this series of bets the profit would have been increased by over 9%. (Obviously, in the table figures have been rounded up or down to the nearest pound.)

You'll notice how the stake never drops below its previous level. Because of this the bank will survive a maximum of twenty consecutive losers. (Losing runs of this magnitude may happen occasionally and punters need be aware of this fact – they are part of the ups and downs of gambling!)

However, a useful way of employing this money management idea is to cut out and start again once a certain profit level has been reached. In the series of bets in the table, stopping once the original £1,000 bank had increased by 75% would have seen the stake revert to £50 after the third 4/1 winner. This is one way of not having the original bank wiped out by twenty consecutive losers.

Note: When using any of the/ form analysis methods from chapter 3 you will find most of the dogs selected will be around the 6/4 – 4/1 mark. Hence, the price range of the winners in the table is reflective of what a punter enjoying a 'hot streak' might encounter.

Method 5

Method 5 is an idea based upon ploughing profits back into your betting. However, this method is a cautious one and very quickly reverts back to base stakes. Particularly suitable for use with a selection method that throws up only a small number of bets, it is designed to run on a meeting to meeting basis. It works like this.

- Put aside an amount of money as a betting bank.
- Set the per-selection stake for the first meeting.
- If you lose at the first meeting, stick to the same stake for the next one.
- If you win, take note of the profit figure and divide it by two.

- Once your selections have been finalised for the next meeting, divide the halved profit figure from the last meeting by the number of selections at the new one.
- Add the resultant figure to the stake set in the second step. This figure will be the per-selection stake for the new meeting.
- Carry out the same procedure after every winning meeting. However, whenever a losing meeting is encountered revert back to the staking figure from the second step.
- When, or if, the bank grows by a pre-determined amount, work out a fresh staking figure and start again.

This might seem a long-winded and cautious way to go about your betting but it does allow you to play up profits and should mean any hot streaks are taken full advantage of. It also means at least half the profits from any one winning meeting are banked. This idea could be used in conjunction with method 1 – i.e. stop betting after a certain number of winners have been found.

In practice the system is simple to operate but let's look at a quick example.

- £1,000 betting bank.
- £40 per-selection stake figure for the first meeting.
- First meeting results in a loss, so £40 remains as the base stake for next meeting.

Or

- Win, for example, £100 at the first meeting. Divide by two to arrive at £50.
- Next meeting sees 5 selections. Divide the £50 by 5 to arrive at £10.
- Add the £10 onto the base stake figure of £40. Thus, £50 is the new per-selection stake.

Method 6

This final method is a more sophisticated from of method 5. It's very much designed to work with shorter-priced selections – i.e. favourites or second favourites.

Rules as follows:

- Set a betting bank.
- Set an initial stakes per selection figure.
- After each ten bets, look at the state of profit or loss.

If a loss is being shown, continue with the original stakes.
If a profit is being shown, do the following:

- If profit is at least 6 times the original stakes, add half of the original stakes amount to subsequent bets.
- If profit is at least 12 times the original stakes, double the original stakes and use the resultant figure for subsequent bets.
- If profit is at least 18 times the original stakes, multiply the original stakes by one and a half and use the resultant figure for subsequent bets.

If, after each series of ten bets, the profit has not reached a figure 6 times the starting stakes, revert <u>right</u> back to the original stake. Obviously, also do the same thing if a loss has been suffered.

When, or if, the betting bank grows to a pre-determined figure, work out a fresh staking figure and start again.

In practice the method looks like this:

- Betting bank £1,000.
- Initial stakes per bet figure of £40
- After ten bets, profit is £180. This is not 6 times the original stakes per bet figure so next ten bets remain staked at £40 each.

Or

- After ten bets, profit is £300. This is 6 times the original stakes per selection figure, so next ten bets staked at £60 each.
- After twenty bets, profit is £500. This is 12 times the original stakes so next ten bets staked at £80 each.

And so on…

The key to this method is reviewing your profit or loss figure after ten bets – and then adhering to the increase / decrease in profits as required.

Ten Golden Rules for Successful Greyhound Race Betting

In the preceding chapters of this book we've examined many aspects of greyhound racing, from selection methods and reading the form through to money management systems. To end the advice – and there has been a lot given – let's consider ten golden rules for successful greyhound race betting.

However, there is one final thing to note. All the ideas and suggestions in this book are not the only ways to find winners at the dog track. There is nothing to stop them serving as the basis for your own methods and systems.

One thing is for sure though, any punter who dismisses the rules that follow will lessen their chances of making a long-term profit from greyhound-race betting – regardless of whether they are following the sport in either Great Britain or anywhere else in the world.

Rule 1: Never bet more than you can afford to lose

This sounds boring and you will have heard it before. Nevertheless, it must be stated again because it's so important. In fact, perhaps the rule should really read 'Never bet more than you can cheerfully afford to lose'. The cheerfully has been missed out though because punters should never be happy about losing any amount, no matter how large or small. However, regardless of being happy or unhappy you really must never bet more than you can afford to lose.

If you start losing more than you can afford to, it will probably lead to unfortunate repercussions in other aspects of your life. But apart from that, you'll also find your judgement becoming distorted. As a result, you'll start backing the wrong dogs and then a vicious circle will start up. So, do not bet more than you can afford to lose. Do not, do not, do not!

Rule 2: Decide on a form analysis or selection method

When you have done this, stick with it. In other words, once you've decided upon – or even developed for yourself – a form analysis or selection method, give it a decent run. Don't chop and change methods because by doing so you'll never develop a feel for the kind of greyhounds that a particular system highlights.

You'll also find that you won't become practised at using any particular method. This is important to remember because you won't want to be spending vast amounts of time scoring up races. No matter how useful you find the form analysis methods, it will be form study that is the most important thing – so save as much time as possible for that.

Rule 3: Study the form carefully

Anyone who starts backing greyhounds on a serious basis will soon be surprised at the amount of time they'll need to put in on form study. At some meetings selections will leap off the page but at others it will be very hard to uncover any decent clues. In fact, you'll often find yourself spending considerable time studying races only to find no selection can be made. Because of this, you must condition yourself to study the form carefully.

Through careful form study you'll quickly be able to identify the races where no worthwhile bets exist. You'll also prevent the situation arising where you've decided on a number of bets, begun placing them, and then realised you've missed a previous winner because you didn't read the form properly. Unfortunately, it does happen and there is nothing more disheartening.

Rule 4: Make decisive selections

This is important. If you can't be decisive over a selection you shouldn't back it. However, this doesn't mean you should only back dogs that you feel are certain to win. There is nothing wrong with selecting greyhounds that have a less than obvious chance of winning. Backing outsiders or dogs that appear to have a better chance than their price suggests is no bad thing. But once you've made a selection it's crucial to stick with it.

Changing your mind just before the off is to be avoided at all costs. It's easier said than done though because everyone has suffered last minute doubts over a selection. But for every occasion a punter has switched away from a loser and on to a winner, there's probably been three times it's gone the other way.

It really is essential to make decisive selections and then stick with them. As an aid to the latter, once your form study is complete, why not make a brief note of the reasons you have made your selections?

Rule 5: Do not bet on emotion

This is a real big one. Placing bets for emotional reasons is the way to certain failure. With dog racing, punters will experience plenty of times when they really want to back something for all the wrong reasons. Why? Simply because they will often have a selection meet trouble in running and appear an unlucky loser. Consequently, they will be determined to back that dog next time out. But, come that next appearance, they will do so without any due consideration as to whether it has a winning chance – or regardless if the race looks to be a better opportunity for another dog.

Equally so, if a greyhound has done you a good turn you might feel tempted to follow it for another race or two. The simple advice is do not. Not unless you have weighed up the new race in a completely calculating manner and are sure your dog is the best bet again.

Rule 6: Keep a record of all your bets

Absolutely essential this one. You must keep at least a record of your profit and loss. In the previous chapter we considered a number of money-management / staking plans. All of them depended on a record of each bet being kept. So, you will not be able to use any of those ideas unless this latest rule is adhered to.

Ideally though, you shouldn't only be recording your profits and losses. Keeping precise details of every bet will stand you in good stead. Take a note of bet type, odds obtained, time of bet and – probably most important of all – the reasons why you placed it. The last point may appear odd but through regularly looking back at previous bets you'll come to know what works for you and what doesn't.

Rule 7: Learn from your mistakes

Yet another essential one. Quite simply, learn to appreciate when your judgement was awry and you backed the wrong dog. Then, avoid doing it again. Of course, from time to time everyone makes bad selections but most don't learn from them.

This will particularly apply when you are suffering a bad run. At times like these you'll often feel disillusioned and your form study will probably suffer as a result. When this happens, you must avoid picking dogs just because they are either the favourite or a long price. Think back to the times you've done it before and take heed. Remember that avoiding losers is a very important part of professional greyhound race betting.

Rule 8: Avoiding a loser is better than missing a winner

This ties in with the previous rule. If you are undecided about whether to back a dog or not, err on the side of caution. Quite simply, if you don't back a dog that then goes on to win you will still have the same amount of cash as you did before the race. But if you back it and it is beaten you will most definitely be worse off! Try and remember this because it will almost certainly save you money in the long-term.

Rule 9: Set up a betting bank

If you adhere to the earlier rule of only betting what you can afford to lose you'll easily be able to set up a bank purely for punting.

A betting bank will make it easier to separate your punting from the other aspects of your life. This is crucial. Any serious attempt at professional greyhound-race betting will be helped by the need to constantly work out whether you can afford to carry on or not. If a betting bank is set up you'll only have to refer to that to know exactly where you stand.

Rule 10: Enjoy your betting

The moment your greyhound betting becomes a chore it's time to stop. Only carry on backing greyhounds while you enjoy doing so. A punter who has become bored with the process of race scoring, form study, selection and then putting bets on will soon start to lose. However, apart from the foolishness of persisting with something that loses you money, why continue when you are not enjoying it?

If you have any doubts over this, visit your local track and take a careful look at some of the die-hards. You'll soon see the ones there only out of habit. The years of losing money – make no mistake, something that will have happened to most – will have taken its toll on them. But, so ingrained will be the habit of going to the track, they will keep turning up, kept going by the occasional winner or successful forecast.

If you ever feel this is happening to you, stop betting immediately.

Directory of Greyhound Racing Terms and Abbreviations

Great Britain and USA

All the Way: Never headed, led all the way

Back Straight: The part of the track opposite to the home straight

Baulked: Impeded by another dog

Blocked: Shut off when trying to move through field (USA equivalent of Baulked)

Box to Wire: Led throughout the race (USA equivalent of All the Way)

Bumped: Hit by another dog

Break: Greyhounds emerging from the traps

Calculated Time: In GB, time of all the other dogs except the winner. Calculated through adding .08 of a second per length (or fraction of) to the winning time depending on how far behind the winner each dog came

Came Again: Made ground up after dropping back

Checked: Hesitated or Propped – shortened stride during race

Closed Fast: Finished fast (USA equivalent of Finished Well)

Close Quarters: Dogs racing close together

Contender: A greyhound thought to have a favourites chance of finishing in the first three

Crowded: When a greyhound has been unable to stride out because other runners are in the way

Did Not Finish: When a greyhound does not complete a race or a trial

Drew Away:	Increased lead in home straight
Early Pace:	The ability of a greyhound to run fast in the earlier parts of a race
Every Chance:	When a greyhound has been able to run unimpeded throughout a race
Faded:	Dropped Back
Fast Away:	Quick out of the traps
Form:	Record of past performances
Front Runner:	A greyhound that tends to always race in the front of its field
Going:	The state of a track's running surface for any given race or meeting
Going Away:	Same as Drew Away
Green:	Inexperienced
Handily:	Win without being pressed, without too much effort
Home Straight:	The final part of a race
Impeded:	General term to describe when a dog has been prevented from giving its true running, through being bumped or baulked etc.
Knocked Back:	Forced back after collision with another runner
Left:	Leave the traps very slowly behind the rest of the field
Length:	Meaning the length of an average greyhound. Used to measure distances between finishing positions
Maiden:	Dog that has never won a race
Middle Pace:	When a greyhound shows good speed in the middle part of a race
Neck:	The third most minimum winning distance in greyhound racing
Miss the break:	When a greyhound leaves the traps behind all the other runners
No Factor:	Trailing the field, never in any real contention
Off Colour:	When a greyhound doesn't run because it has shown signs of being unwell

Off-strided:	Momentarily loses, or has to reduce, stride or balance
Outrun:	Good effort but unable to keep pace with other dogs
Place:	2nd place in a race
Pinched Back:	Crowded and forced to drop back
Quick Away:	When a greyhound runs fast straight from the starting traps
Race Comments:	A description of a greyhound's race performance
Rough Trip:	Crowded, blocked or baulked several times in a race
Rail Runner:	Dog that runs tight to the inside rail (USA equivalent of Railer)
Saved Ground:	Raced on the inside, near the rail
Season Suppressed:	When a bitch has her natural season suppressed with drugs
Sectional Placings:	The position in the field a greyhound held at pre-defined stages of a race
Short Head:	The minimum winning distance in greyhound racing
Show:	3rd place in an eight-dog race
Shuffled Back:	To be so crowded and impeded as to lose considerable ground
Slow Starter:	A greyhound who always emerges slowly from the traps
Stayer:	A greyhound able to sustain racing speed over distances of about 600 metres plus (3/8 mile in USA)
Stretch Drive:	Extra effort in the home straight
Strip:	Racing Track surface
Trailed:	Run at the rear of the field
Trial:	What greyhounds run in as preparation for proper races
Waiting:	When a greyhound appears not to want to run past an opponent

Weakened:	Not being able to sustain effort after showing good early speed
Wide Runner:	A dog that runs wide at the bends
Wire:	The finishing line

Terms Exclusive to USA

1/8th Call:	The position of a dog at the 1/8th mile mark in a USA race.
Actual Running Time:	A greyhound's individual finishing time in a race.
Average Speed:	Average amount of time in seconds it takes a greyhound to complete a race relative to the track record. This is calculated through the last three finish times being added, divided by three and then subtracting the average from the track record and multiplying by ten. A zero is the best score possible.
Back Runner:	A greyhound that always tends to race at the rear of its field
Box Bias:	A trap number showing a distinct advantage or disadvantage in terms of number of races recently won.
Break Call:	The call made just as the greyhounds leave the starting traps
Class:	See Effective Grade
Closing Ability:	The ability of a greyhound to perform best in the latter parts of race. This is calculated through adding the 1/8th call from a greyhound's last six races, dividing them by six, and then subtracting this average from the average of the last six finish calls
Effective Grade:	The grade that reflects a greyhound's current running ability, regardless of current race designation. Also referred to as class.

Finish Call or	
Final Call:	The position of a greyhound at the end of a race.
Inside Runner:	A greyhound that tends to race toward the rail or inside of the track
Kennel Rating:	A numeric classification denoting kennel quality
Outside Runner:	A greyhound that tends to race toward the outside of the track
Schooling Race:	A race with no grade attached to it. Where greyhounds run to be prepared for future contests (the Great Britain equivalent is a Trial)
Start Call:	The position of a greyhound at the start of the race after it emerges from the traps
Stretch Call:	The position of a greyhound as the home straight is entered
Track Condition:	A description of the track's running surface during a given race
Winner's Time:	The winning greyhound's individual finish time in a race

Great Britain: Common Racecard Abbreviations

A:	Always
Aw:	Away
B:	Badly
Blk:	Baulked
Bmp:	Bumped
Br:	British Bred
Brk:	Break
Calc:	Calculated
Chl:	Challenged

Clr:	Clear
CmAg:	Came Again
Crd:	Crowded
DH:	Dead Heat
Dis:	Distance
Disq:	Disqualified
DNF:	Did Not Finish
Drpd:	Dropped
E:	Early
EvCh:	Every Chance
Ext:	Extra
F:	Favourite
Fd:	Faded
Fight:	Fought
Fin:	Finished
Fr:	From
GR:	Graded Race
H:	Hurdles
Hcp:	Handicap
HndTm:	Hand Timed
Imp:	Impeded
J:	Joint-Favourite
Lck:	Lacked
Lm:	Lame
(M):	In GB open races only, Middle Runner
Mid:	Middle
N:	Normal
Nk:	Neck
O/C:	Off Colour
Outp:	Outpaced
P:	Pace
QA:	Quick Away
(R):	In GB open races only, Rails Runner

Rec:	Record (as in track record)
ReRn:	Rerun
Rls:	Railed
RnIn:	Run-In
RnUp:	Run-Up
Rst:	Rest
S:	Slow (Away etc)
SA:	Slow Away
Schl:	Schooling
Scr:	Scratch
SH:	Short Head
SP:	Starting Price
SPl:	Sectional Placings
Ssn:	Season
SsnSup:	Season Suppressed
Stb:	Stumbled
Styd:	Stayed
Th'out:	Throughout
Tk:	Track
Tm:	Time
(W):	Wide Runner
Wtg:	Waiting

The Hall Of Fame

SIX GREYHOUNDS that, in their day, set the tracks alight. As you get to know the sport, perhaps you'll come to form your own view concerning what other dogs should have been put into The Hall of Fame.

Mick The Miller: (Ir. and GB) The first superstar of the sport. Ran during the late 1920's and early 1930's.

Ballyregan Bob: (GB) A star of the 1980s. Held the world record for consecutive wins.

Chief Havoc: (Aus) Australia's first star greyhound that remains a legend in racing circles down under.

Joe Dump: (USA) Took the world record for consecutive wins off Ballyregan Bob.

Real Huntsman: (USA) A star from the USA from an earlier era.

Scurlogue Champ: (GB) A marathon distance dog who had the most amazing running style that simply can't be described in words. Try and find a video of him and you'll see what we mean!

Belle Vue (Manchester)

General manager: John R Gilburn
Racing manager: Mick Smith
Telephone for enquiries: Enquiries 0161 223 8000
Restaurant 0161 223 6060
Fax 0161 223 8432
Email Address: bvraceoffice@gralimited.co.uk
Website Address: http://www.bellevuestadium.co.uk
Directions to track: Follow signs to city centre, then take A57 signs for Hyde and Sheffield. Belle Vue is signposted and is ten minutes drive from city centre. Rail: Manchester Piccadilly or Victoria,10 minute taxi ride to track.
Race Days: Tuesday, Thursday, Friday and Saturday.
Admission Prices: £4.00 Tuesday, Thursday and Friday, £5.00 Saturday.
Crowd capacity: 4,100
Car parking capacity: 400
Six Pack Details: Tuesday, Thursday, Friday and Saturday - minimum of 10.
Catering Facilities Main restaurant. Fast food bars. Buffet menu. Full restaurant facilities. Five bars featuring live sport on 21 TV's plus large screen.
Corporate Facilities: Two executive suites available with private bar, tote and race video facilities (maximum capacity of 225).
Sponsorship packages range from £250 - £2,000 and are tailored to individual needs.
Restaurant Facilities: 418 seat restaurant serving A La Carte and party menu, as well as regular seasonal special offers.

Snack facilities: Two modern fast food bars.bars.

Racing Info

Distance raced: 237, 465, 465H, 647, 875 metres.

Track circumference: 395 metres.

Run To First Bend: 103 metres (465m)

72.50 metres (647m)

Track Records: 237m Parliament Act 14.25 - 08/03/01

465m Upade Joe 27.37 - 11/05/00

465mH Born to Go 28.15 - 24/07/01

647m Drumsna Cross 39.53 - 10/08/00

647mH El Tenor 41.06 - 18/05/99

875m Let Us Know 54.50 - 23/10/01

Hare Type Outside Swaffham

Major Open Events: The Strongbow Cider Gorton Cup (March)

The Dransfield Stayers (March)

The Belle Vue Bookmakers Northern Oaks (April)

The Benholmes Northern Flat (May)

The Wafcol Cock O'The North (July))

The Carling Manchester Puppy Cup (September)

The Carling Stayers Grand (September)

The William Hill Laurels (October)

Brighton and Hove

General manager: Stuart Walton

Racing manager: Peter Miller

Telephone for enquiries: 01273 204601

Restaurant 08457 023952

Email Address: hove.stadium@coral.co.uk

Website Address: http://www.trap6.com/hove/index.htm

Directions to track: From London, M23 to A23 (virtually motorway throughout), big new roundabout with Q8 garage on the right. Take the road up the hill so garage remains on the right. At the top of the hill, go straight on at the roundabout, following signs for Hove. Take second turning on the left, stadium is 200 yards on the left. Rail: Hove Station (Victoria - Littlehampton main line service) taxi 5 minutes, or from Brighton Station, taxi 10 minutes.

Race Days: Tuesday, Thursday and Saturday evenings. Wednesday and Sunday afternoons.

Admission Prices: Weekdays £4.00, Saturday £5.00 (including racecard). Wednesday and Sunday afternoons free.

Crowd capacity: 2,200

Car parking capacity: 365

Six Pack Details: Tuesday, Thursday (£12) and Saturday (£15) - minimum of 6.

Catering Facilities Restaurant. Two fast food grills. Five licensed bars.

Corporate Facilities: Race and non-race day facilities available.

Restaurant Facilities: Restaurant (capacity 450) with A La Carte menu and chefs special menu.

Snack facilities: Snacks available from fast food grills.

Racing Info

Distance raced: 285, 475, 515, 695, 740, 930, 970 metres.

Track circumference: 455 metres.

Run To First Bend: 105 metres (4 bends)

50 metres (6 bends)

Track Records: 285m Smoking Jonesey 16.29 - 09/06/01

475m Farmhouse Gold 27.48 - 30/03/02
515m Windgap Java 29.56 - 09/06/01
515mH Group Tycoon 30.78 - 24/07/01
695m Form Of Magic 40.82 - 26/03/02
740m Form Of Magic 43.59 - 22/05/01
930m Kegans Gold 56.68 - 24/07/01
970m Marys Gem 59.56 14/09/97
Hare Type Swaffham
Major Open Events: The Courage Greyhound Olympic
Chas Miller Sussex Cup
The Regency

Brough Park (Newcastle)

General manager: Kenneth Little
Racing manager: Ian Hillis/Terry Meynell
Telephone for enquiries: 0191 265 8011
Email Address: newcastle@broughparkdogs.fsnet.co.uk
Website Address: http://www.newcastlebroughparkgreyhounds.co.uk
Directions to track: From Newcastle city centre, follow A193 towards Wallsend for two miles. Rail: Main line Newcastle station. Metro to Chillingham, then five minute walk or taxi from station.
Race Days: Tuesday, Friday and Saturday.
Admission Prices: £4.00 (Information on special deals for groups or parties etc. available on request by telephoning 0191 265 8011)
Crowd capacity: 1,000
Car parking capacity: 300 plus
Six Pack Details: Tuesday, Friday and Saturday - minimum of 10.
Catering Facilities Restaurant seating 125 Guests.
Corporate Facilities: Fossway banqueting suite for up to 200.
Restaurant Facilities: 125 seats.
Snack facilities: Upstairs bar area.

Racing Info

Distance raced: 480, 500, 640 metres.
Track circumference: 415 metres.
Run To First Bend: 130 metres (480m)
58 metres (640m)
Track Records: 290m Cloncuryy Flyer 16.92 - 13/12/01
460m New Level 27.81 - 12/05/92
480m Over The Pike 28.54 - 17/11/01
480m handicap Dinn Re Prince 28.94 - 09/10/99
480mH Ballyhane Rio 30.10 - 18/09/01
480mH handicap Ballyhane Rio 30.18 - 09/12/00
500m Littlemoor Larry 29.97 - 31/07/95

500m handicap Official Sail 30.24 - 20/03/99
500mH handicap Jenks Challenger 31.33 07/09/91
640m Wath Apache 39.08 - 13/12/01
640m handicap Village Star 39.50 - 19/08/94
670m handicap Breathless 42.00 - 20/06/92
825m Let Us Know 51.55 - 12/04/01
895m Give Her Time 56.67 - 23/06/98
Hare Type Outside Sumner
Major Open Events: All England Cup (September)

Catford (London)

General manager: Stan Wolfe
Racing manager: Derek Hope
Telephone for enquiries: 020 8690 8000
Racing Office 020 8690 2240
Email Address: raceoffice@gralimited.co.uk
Website Address: http://www.catfordstadium.co.uk
Directions to track: GRA Ltd, Catford Stadium, Catford Bridge, London, SE6 4RJ. Situated adjacent to South Circular Road between Catford and Catford Bridge Stations.
Race Days: Thursday, Friday and Saturday evenings. Tuesday afternoons.
Admission Prices: £4.50 adults, £2.00 concessions, £2.00 children under 14.
Crowd capacity: 4,810
Car parking capacity: 400
Six Pack Details: Thursday, Friday and Saturday - minimum of 6.
Catering Facilities Five public bars, three fast food counters. Restaurant, Diner and one Hospitality suite.
Corporate Facilities: Entertainment lounge for up to 150 guests.
Restaurant Facilities: 164 seats. Chefs Menu and A La Carte.
Snack facilities: Three fast food counters.

Racing Info

Distance raced: 222, 385, 385H, 555, 718, 888 metres.
Track circumference: 333 metres.
Run To First Bend: 75 metres (385m)
80 metres (555m)
Track Records: 222m Im From Tallow 13.56 - 14/07/90
385m Union Decree 23.20 - 04/07/98
385mH Kildare Slippy 23.73 - 18/05/91
555m Rio Shadow 34.41 - 09/05/98
555mH El Tenor 35.15 - 27/05/99
718m Scurlogue Champ 45.58 - 20/10/84

888m Scurlogue Champ 57.60 - 19/06/86
Hare Type Outside Swaffham type McGee
Major Open Events: William Hill Greenwich Cup (April)
Scurry Cup (June)
William Hill Gold Collar (September)
Boxing Day Marathon (December)

Crayford

General manager: Barry Stanton
Racing manager: Harry Bull
Telephone for enquiries: 01322 557836
Racing Office 01322 522262
Email Address: racingoffice@crayforddogs.demon.co.uk
Website Address: http://www.crayford.com
Directions to track: M25, junction 1. Take A2 and follow signs to Crayford. Track is on large new one-way system in town centre. Rail: Crayford Station which is adjacent to the track.
Race Days: Monday and Saturday evenings, first race 7.30pm. Tuesday and Thursday afternoons (start times vary) and Saturday mornings.
Admission Prices: £4.50 Adults, £3.00 Children. Tuesday and Thursday BAGS - free entry and racecard. Saturday BAGS - free entry.
Crowd capacity: 1,200
Car parking capacity: 800
Six Pack Details: Monday - minimum of four, and Saturday - minimum of 10.
Catering Facilities Luxury restaurant seating 216. Snack bar. 2 lounge bars.
Corporate Facilities: Club suite with private facilities for up to 50 people.
Restaurant Facilities: 216-seat luxury restaurant.
Snack facilities: Snack bar serving wide range of basket meals, beverages etc.

Racing Info

Distance raced: 380, 540, 714, 874, 1048 metres.
Track circumference: 334 metres.
Run To First Bend: 77 metres (380m)
77 metres (540m)
Track Records: 380m Chasing A Dream 23.18 - 05/03/02
380mH Dynamic Display 23.70 - 30/12/95
540m Side Wink 33.46 - 09/01/93
540mH El Tenor 34.16 - 13/04/98

714m Blues Best Tayla 45.19 - 24/02/01
874m Clonbrin Black 56.15 - 16/10/93
1048m Stansted Flyer 69.81 - 07/09/96
Hare Type Swaffham
Major Open Events: Ladbroke Golden Jacket (February)
Countrywide Steel and Tubes Vase (June)
Countrywide Steel and Tubes Guys & Dolls (September)
Tony Morris & John Humphreys Flying Four (September)
Kent St Leger (October)

Hall Green (Birmingham)

General manager: Stephen Rea
Racing manager: Gary Woodward
Telephone for enquiries: 0870 840 7000
Restaurant 0870 840 7437
Email Address: stephenrea@gralimited.co.uk
Website Address: http://www.hallgreenstadium.co.uk
Directions to track: Four miles south of Birmingham city centre, off A34 into York Road. Track signposted and approx. 400 yards along York Road. Rail: Main line New Street Birmingham, taxi or local trains to Hall Green Station. GRA Ltd York Road Hall Green Birmingham B28 8LQ
Race Days: Tuesday, Friday and Saturday evenings.
Admission Prices: £4.00 Lower Grandstand, £5.00 Upper Grandstand.
Crowd capacity: 3,000
Car parking capacity: 600
Six Pack Details: Tuesday, Friday and Saturday - any number of guests.
Catering Facilities Two main restaurants. Buffet area, fast food facilities.
Corporate Facilities: Four executive boxes 24 covers in each – interconnecting.
Conference Facilities: Facilities in The Blue Riband Suite.
Restaurant Facilities: Table 'D' Hote and party menus.
Snack facilities: Fast food bar.

Racing Info

Distance raced: 258, 480, 645, 670, 820, 892 metres.
Track circumference: 412 metres.
Run To First Bend: 85 metres (480m)
Track Records: 258m Hows Yer Man 15.32 - 28/05/93
480m Westmead Chick 28.20 - 19/11/94
480m Vintage Cleaner 28.20 - 25/04/00
480mH Kildare Slippy 28.52 - 08/04/92
645m Palace Issue 39.01 - 22/09/00
645mH Eezar Ferrari 40.71 - 13/12/99

870m Fearless Lynx 40.44 - 04/02/95
892m Spenwood Wizard 55.34 - 16/06/00
Hare Type Swaffham McGee
Major Open Events: The William Hill Blue Riband (April)
The Suite Ideas Gymcrack Puppy Championship (August)
The Breeders Forum Produce Stakes (October)
The William Hill Midland Flat Championship (November)

Harlow

General manager: Toni Nicholls
Racing manager: Mark Schellenberg
Telephone for enquiries: 01279 426804
Directions to track: From M11, take A414 - track tourist signed from there. From A10, take A414.
Race Days: Wednesday, Friday and Saturday evenings. First race at 7.30pm. Boxing Day, first race 11am. Easter Sunday, first race 2.00pm.
Admission Prices: £4.50 inc. racecard, pensioners £2.50.
Crowd capacity: 1,500
Car parking capacity: 400
Six Pack Details: All nights - minimum of six and must be pre-booked
Catering Facilities Fast food and traditional bar meals.
Corporate Facilities: Available on request.
Restaurant Facilities: For party bookings only.
Snack facilities: Club Room Bar.

Racing Info

Distance raced: 238, 415, 592, 769, 946 metres.
Track circumference: 354 metres.
Track Records: 238m Quiet Cheer 14.81 - 21/12/97
415m Eds Cash 25.72 - 20/08/99
415m Corrough Power 25.72 - 01/01/00
415mH Simply Speedy 26.33 - 03/10/01
592m Decoy Cheetah 37.13 - 16/06/95
592m Treasured Manx 37.13 - 18/10/95
592mH Bozy Blue Blaze 39.63 - 13/05/01
769m Micks Best Magic 49.59 - 09/01/02
946m Souda Bay 63.14 - 13/04/98
Hare Type Outside Swaffham
Major Open Events: £750 competition every week (415 & 592m alternatively)

Henlow Greyhound Stadium

General manager: Tony McDonnell

Racing manager: Keith Mellor

Telephone for enquiries: 01462 851 850

Fax: 01462 815593

Email Address: henlowgreyhounds@clara.co.uk

Website Address: http://www.henlowdogs.co.uk

Directions to track: From A1 and M1, take Luton turn off to Hitchin. From Hitchin, take A600 towards Bedford for about 6 miles. Track is on this road, on the left and opposite Henlow Camp.

Rail: Hitchin Station, 10 minute taxi ride to the stadium.

Henlow Stadium Bedford Road Henlow Camp Lower Stondon Bedfordshire SG16 6EA

Race Days: Mondays and Fridays (7.30pm). Trials on Wednesday evenings 7.30pm (free admission).

Admission Prices: £4.50 Monday. £4.50 Fridays (open race night). Children under 14-years-old free.

Crowd capacity: 600

Car parking capacity: 1,000

Six Pack Details: Monday and Friday - minimum of 10.

Catering Facilities Fast food bar and licensed bar (Intertrack betting via satellite).

Racing Info

Distance raced: 250, 460, 550, 660, 870, 960 metres.

Track circumference: 413 metres.

Track Records: 250m Gamble It 14.96 - 01/05/00

460m Couriers Dream 27.42 - 18/09/98

550m Westmead Baron 33.43 - 12/04/01

660m Lobo 40.21 - 15/10/99

870m Tiptree Poker 55.31 - 27/10/97

Hare Type Outside Swaffham

Major Open Events: Carlsberg Tetley Challenge (September)

Open races every Monday - 460m puppy, 460m maiden, 550m maiden, 660m
Open races every Friday - 250m, 460m, 550m, 660m

Hull

General manager: Gary Ince

Racing manager: David Gray

Telephone for enquiries: 01482 374131

Email Address: hulldogs@clara.co.uk

Website Address: http://www.hull-greyhounds.co.uk

Directions to track: Craven Park Stadium, Preston Road, Hull, HU9 5HE. From M62, via A63 (under the Humber Bridge) keep on the Clive Sullivan Way (dual carriageway), over twisting flyover into Castle Street past the marina, straight through all traffic lights into Garrison Road and over the River Hull (Myton Bridge). At the first roundabout, take the second exit (towards docks and Hedon), along the dual carriageway. At the second roundabout, take the third exit onto Hedon Road, continue for approx. two miles until passing the first entrance for King George Dock and North Sea Ferries. Continue under railway bridge (100 yards) and, at the next set of major traffic lights, turn left into Marfleet Lane (ring road). Over the flyover, turn right at the next major set of traffic lights (crossroads), then turn right onto Preston Road (dual carriageway) before taking a right 600 yards further along (opposite the cemetery). Drive past the supermarket and into the main car park of Craven Park. Rail: Hull Station, short taxi ride to stadium.

Race Days: Thursday and Saturday.

Admission Prices: £4.50 including racecard.

Car parking capacity: Approx 150

Six Pack Details: Not available.

Catering Facilities £6.00 deal includes entrance, racecard, chicken or scampi and chips.

£11.00 Carvery includes entrance, racecard, carvery meal, glass of wine and £1.00 tote voucher.

Restaurant Facilities: 80 covers. Carvery on Saturday, normal menu on Thursday.

Racing Info

Distance raced: 240, 460, 490, 655, 875 metres.

Track circumference: 415 metres.

Run To First Bend: 90 metres (490m)

Track Records: 240m Curaghator Lad 14.71 - 12/05/98

460m Ferndale Scholar 28.26 - 05/10/96

490m Andys Surprise 30.03 - 02/05/96

655m Fearsome Misty 41.24 - 05/10/96

705m Dalcash Duke 44.98

875m Spenwood Gem 57.37 - 15/07/01

1070m Ridgefield Dream 72.00 - 10/04/97

Hare Type Fannon Swaffham

Major Open Events: The Hull Derby (July)

Kinsley

General manager: John Curran
Racing manager: Craig Hunt
Telephone for enquiries: 01977 610946
Email Address: kinsleygreyhound@clara.co.uk
Website Address: http://www.kinsleydogs.co.uk
Directions to track: 96, Wakefield Road, Kinsley. Near Pontefract. The stadium is situated south east of Wakefield, a few miles from the stately home and grounds of Nostell Priory.
Race Days: Tuesday, Friday and Saturday (7.30pm). Occasional Sunday (7pm)
Admission Prices: £3.60 (OAPS and 14-16year-olds £2.60)
Crowd capacity: 3,000
Car parking capacity: 300
Six Pack Details: Tuesday, Friday and Saturday
Catering Facilities Jubilee Restaurant (seats 100)
Jubilee Bistro (seats 60)
Kinsley Buffet
Restaurant Facilities: Jubilee Restaurant seats 100

Racing Info

Distance raced: 275, 450, 485, 656, 866 metres.
Track circumference: 380 metres
Track Records: 275m Harsu Prince 16.65 - 25/09/01
450m Farloe Careless 27.46 - 24/03/00
485m Pack Them In 29.03 - 258/09/01
656m Frisby Fassan 41.33 - 25/09/01
866m Spenwood Wizard 53.32 - 28/05/00
Hare Type Outside Swaffham

Mildenhall

General manager: Terry Waters

Racing manager: Mike Hill

Telephone for enquiries: 01638 711777

Directions to track: From the A11 'Fiveways' roundabout at Barton Mills, take the A1101 to Mildenhall, go straight over the first roundabout, the first set of traffic lights and the first set of pedestrian lights. At the second roundabout take the first left, then the first right (sign posts West Row). Follow until you reach a T junction, turn left, then first right. The stadium is situated one and a half miles on left hand side. Rail: Nearest station is Ely.

Race Days: Monday and Friday evenings, first race 7.30pm.

Admission Prices: £4.00 (including racecard)

Crowd capacity: 8,000

Car parking capacity: 5,000

Restaurant Facilities: Seats 80. With tote betting facilities, race video screens. Varied menus with vegetarian and children sections. Fully licensed.

Snack facilities: Fast food bar serving fish and chips, pies, burgers, chicken.

Racing Info

Distance raced: 220, 375, 545, 700, 870, 1025 metres.

Track circumference: 325 metres.

Run To First Bend: 70 metres (375m)

Track Records: 220m Lots of Jolly 13.39 - 26/10/93

375m Flashy Beo 22.88 - 11/10/96

545m Lady Small Paws 33.76 - 26/02/01

700m Trade Link 44.44 - 07/10/99

VICTOR KNIGHT

870m Barwise Smiler 56.15 - 28/09/98
1025m Dust Image 67.49 - 16/11/94
Hare Type Outside Sumner

Milton Keynes

General manager: Susan Conway

Racing manager: Bill Johnson

Telephone for enquiries: 01908 670150

Email Address: info@stadiauk.com

Website Address: http://www.mkgreyhounds.com

Directions to track: M1 northbound, take junction 13, then A421 towards Milton Keynes South. Stadium is situated just past third roundabout. Rail: Bletchley Station or Milton Keynes Central, both 5 minutes from stadium by taxi.

Race Days: Tuesday, Thursday and Saturday evenings. Sunday afternoons.

Admission Prices: £5.00 (OAP's and ladies free on Tuesday and Thursday).

Crowd capacity: 3,000

Car parking capacity: over 3,000

Catering Facilities Restaurants, snack bars, licensed bars. Ice cream vendor in summer.

Corporate Facilities: Restaurant available for corporate events on race days and weekdays.

Restaurant Facilities: 104 covers.

Snack facilities: Snack bar serving hot and cold meals, burgers, chips etc, also sweets.

Racing Info

Distance raced: 245, 440, 620, 815 metres.

Track circumference: 375 metres.

Run To First Bend: 80 metres (440m)

72 metres (620m)

Track Records: 245m Westfield Earl 14.76

440m Broken Quest 26.28 - 21/04/98

440m H Springwell Boost 27.15

620m Cushie Amazing 37.96 - 31/01/98

620m Farloe Bonus 37.96 - 22/08/98
620mH El Tenor 39.21 - 31/08/98
815m Spenwood Gem 51.22 - 24/04/99
995m Gift Of Gold 64.10 - 19/08/00
Hare Type Swaffham McGee
Major Open Events: Milton Keynes Summer Cup (August)
Milton Keynes Derby (November)
Milton Keynes Christmas Cracker (December)

Monmore Green

General manager: Richard Brankley

Racing manager: Jim Woods

Telephone for enquiries: 01902 452648

Website Address: http://www.monmoredogs.co.uk

Directions to track: M6, take junction 10 (A454) Wolverhampton Road, which by-passes Willenhall and continue to the junction with Stow Heath Lane. Stadium is sign posted and behind Wolverhampton wholesale vegetable market off that road. Rail: Wolverhampton Station, buses and taxis to the stadium.

Race Days: Monday and Friday afternoons (BAGS).Thursday and Saturday evenings.

Admission Prices: £4.00 including racecard. BAGS free admission

Crowd capacity: 1,300

Car parking capacity: 400

Catering Facilities 170 seater restaurant, 3 bars. Snack bar with hot and cold food.

Corporate Facilities: Three executive boxes.

Restaurant Facilities: 170-seat trackside restaurant. Tote messenger service - CCTV. Disabled facilities and baby changing room.

Snack facilities: Fast food bar with hot and cold food.

Racing Info

Distance raced: 264, 480, 630, 684, 835, 900 metres.

Track circumference: 419 metres.

Track Records: 210m Cry Havoc 12.64 - 20/03/97

264m Parliament Act 15.32 - 28/08/01

416m Devitos Chance 24.96 - 10/12/97

480m Larkhill Jo 27.95 - 07/07/97

480mH Brave Ruler 28.88 - 26/07/99

630m Slippy Elite 37.81 - 28/11/98

684m True Honcho 41.03 - 14/04/01

835m Spenwood Gem 52.09 - 17/09/98

Knappogue Oak 52.09 - 28/08/01
880m Thornfield Pride 54.79 - 19/07/97
900m Ladys Storm 57.03 - 09/07/98
1104m Travel Now 72.66 - 25/03/00
Hare Type Swaffham
Major Open Events: Puppy Derby (March)
Summer Classic
Gold Cup (July)

Nottingham

General manager: Nathan Corden
Racing manager: Peter Robinson and Richard Munton
Telephone for enquiries: 0115 910 3333
Email Address: nottsdogs@aol.com
Website Address: http://www.nottinghamgreyhoundstadium.com
Directions to track: Three miles from city centre, located next to Colwick park and Nottingham racecourse. Colwick Park is situated on the A612. Rail: Two miles from Midland Station. £3-£4 taxi ride.
Race Days: Monday, Thursday and Saturday. Tuesday afternoon.
Admission Prices: £3.00 Monday and Thursday. £4.00 Saturday. Free Tuesday afternoon.
Crowd capacity: 1,500
Car parking capacity: 1,000
Six Pack Details: Monday, Thursday and Saturday - minimum of 10.
Catering Facilities 250 seater restaurant, snack bar
Corporate Facilities: Corporate packages in Raceview Restaurant
Restaurant Facilities: 250-seat Raceview Restaurant
Snack facilities: Fast food bar.

Racing Info

Distance raced: 300, 480, 500, 700, 722, 902 metres.
Track circumference: 437 metres.
Run To First Bend: 85 metres (500m)
55 metres (700m)
Track Records: 300m Nervous Paddy 17.81 - 24/12/01
480m Tullerboy Lass 28.83 - 12/06/01
500m Top Savings 29.67 - 30/08/01
700m Sexy Delight 42.73 - 11/06/00
722m El Poker 45.38 - 28/08/00
902m Let Us Know 57.25 - 11/03/02
Hare Type Outside Swaffham McGee
Major Open Events: The Victor Chandler Select Stakes (July)

VICTOR KNIGHT

The William Hill Puppy Derby (August)
John Smith Eclipse (November)
The Peter Derrick National Sprint (December)

Oxford

General manager: Mark Beattie

Racing manager: Gary Baiden

Telephone for enquiries: 01865 778 222 ext 201

Email Address: General Manager: Sarahbuy@gralimited.co.uk

Enquiries: oxreserve@gralimited.co.uk

Website Address: http://www.oxfordstadium.co.uk

Directions to track: M40 junction 8 or 9 – follow the ring road towards Cowley. At the BMW motor plant, head towards Watlington on the B480. Take the next right at the traffic lights into Sandy Lane. We are 100 yards on the right hand side of the road.

Rail, Oxford Station (Paddington Line).

Bus, number 1 or 5 picks up at the train station and Oxford town centre.

Race Days: Tuesday, Thursday and Saturday evenings. First race 7.35pm. Friday afternoons and every other Wednesday. For times of afternoon racing please contact the stadium as times may vary.

Admission Prices: £4.50 including racecard. Afternoons free admission and racecard.

Crowd capacity: 1,500

Six Pack Details: Tuesday, Thursday and Saturdays. £10.00 per person, £12.50 per person with guaranteed seating - subject to availability.

Catering Facilities 300 seater Restaurant 180 seater Six-Pack area (extra cost), fast food area, Three bars. Buffet facilities.

Corporate Facilities: Three Executive Suites available. Each suite holds up to 24 people, these can be opened up to accommodate larger parties of up to 48 and 72 people. Executive Suite buffet menus on request. Tote runners at your table with private bar facilities. Excellent viewing facilities.

Restaurant Facilities: Extensive mid-week and Saturday menu in the Grandstand Restaurant. Tote runners and wine waiters at your table.

Snack facilities: Racers and Trappers snack bars, selling a range of burgers, fries, baked potatoes, pies, rolls etc.

Racing Info

Distance raced: 250, 450, 595, 645, 845, 1040 metres.

Track circumference: 395 metres

Run To First Bend: 100 metres (4 bends)

90 metres (6 bends)

Track Records: 250m Debbys Lad 14.96 - 28/10/98

450m Farloe Club 26.57 - 17/03/00

450mH Enjoy Your Luck 27.32 - 18/07/00

595m El Tara 36.78 - 24/07/01

645m Aztec Sun 39.39 - 22/03/98

645mH Bozy Blue Blaze 40.94 - 06/02/01

845m Tralee Crazy 52.16 - 22/03/98

1040m Honeygar Bell 67.63 - 14/11/89

Hare Type Swaffham

Major Open Events: Trafalgar Cup (February)

Pall Mall (March)

Gold Cup

Oxfordshire Trophy

Cesarewitch (November)

Perry Barr (Birmingham)

General manager: Maurice Buckland

Racing manager: Tin Hale

Telephone for enquiries: 0121 356 2324

Restaurant 0121 356 3734

Directions to track: Perry Barr Greyhound Racing Club Ltd Aldridge Road Perry Barr Birmingham B42 2ET. From Birmingham, leave on A324 for the Bull Ring. Join the A34 and then take the A453 under the fly-over. Stadium 100 yards on left. From M6/M5, turn off towards city centre at junction of M6. Follow A34 and fork left at Perry Barr onto A453 (Albridge Road). Large free car park at the stadium. Rail: New Street Station, taxi to stadium.

Race Days: Monday, Tuesday, Thursday, Friday and Saturday evenings from 7.30pm. Wednesday afternoon and most Sundays.

Admission Prices: £4.00 Thursday and Saturday, £3.50 Monday and Friday. Afternoons free.

Crowd capacity: 1,500

Car parking capacity: 400

Six Pack Details: Tuesday, Thursday and Friday - minimum of 10.

Catering Facilities Licensed bar, snack bar, restaurant. Executive boxes and function room.

Corporate Facilities: Restaurant, executive boxes and function room.

Restaurant Facilities: Licensed restaurant, executive boxes and function room.

Racing Info

Distance raced: 275, 480, 660, 710, 895 metres.

Track circumference: 434 metres.

Run To First Bend: 80 metres (4 bends)

50 metres (6 bends)

Track Records: 275m Ancient Heart 16.40 - 15/10/91

460m Velvet Spark 27.67 -01/08/94

480 Derbay Flyer - 25/09/99

500m Toms Lodge 29.94 - 25/09/93
660m Cuba 40.88 - 27/10/01
710m Head For Glory 44.13 - 14/10/99
895 Spenwood Wizard 56.97 - 04/09/00
Hare Type Outside Sumner

Peterborough

General manager: Rob Perkins & Richard Perkins

Racing manager: Con Baker

Telephone for enquiries: 01733 296939

Email Address: info@peterboroughgreyhounds.com

Website Address: http://www.peterboroughgreyhounds.com

Directions to track: A1M (Jct 17) and A47, turn off the ring the ring road (A1139) at exit 5 (brown information signposts to Greyhound Stadium from thereon). Rail: Peterborough Station, 2 miles from track. First Drove Fengate Peterborough

Race Days: Evenings - Tuesday, Wednesday, Friday and Saturday (gates open 6.30, first race 7.30).

Admission Prices: £4.00 (including racecard)

Crowd capacity: 1,500

Car parking capacity: 500 (can accept coaches)

Six Pack Details: Tuesday, Wednesday and Friday £10.00. Saturday £12.00. Minimum of 10.

Catering Facilities Silver Service Restaurant. Fast food grills. Five licensed bars.

Corporate Facilities: Restaurant by arrangement.

Restaurant Facilities: Raceview Restaurant - three-course meal, coffee £16.00 per person Tuesday and Wednesday, £17.00 Friday and Saturday (prices do not include £4.00 entry fee).

Discounts for larger groups - £18.00 per person including entry for 16 or more guests Tuesday and Wednesday, £20.00 Friday and Saturday.

Snack facilities: Snacks available from fast food grill.

Racing Info

Distance raced: 235, 420, 605, 790, 975 metres.

Track circumference: 370 metres.

Run To First Bend: 80 metres (4 bends)

80 metres (6 bends)

Track Records: 235m Mount Royal Fox 14.31 - 19/02/95

420m Highway Leader 25.15 - 30/07/94

420mH Im Henry 25.58 - 17/05/97
605m Glencoes Tom 37.11 - 09/04/02
790m Fortunate Man 49.66 - 15/06/92
975m Lenas Cadet 63.30 - 19/11/88
 Hare Type Outside Swaffham
Major Open Events: Peterborough Marathon
Bass Brewers Cesarewitch
Stoneacre Peterborough Derby
Peterborough Evening Telegraph Puppy Cesarewitch
Wafcol Puppy Derby
Alan Speechley Fengate Collar

Poole

General manager: Richard Evans
Racing manager: Dave Lawrence
Telephone for enquiries: 01202 677449
Racing Office 01202 685107
Email Address: info@stadiauk.com
Website Address: http://www.poolegreyhounds.com
Directions to track: Wimborne Road, Poole, Dorset, BH15 2BP. M3 to M27 and then signposts to Poole town centre. Armdale shopping centre is adjacent to track. Rail: Waterloo to Poole, track 500 yards from station.
Race Days: Tuesday, Thursday and Saturday evenings.
Admission Prices: £5.00 including racecard.
Catering Facilities Snack bar and five licensed bars
Corporate Facilities: Function rooms available.
Restaurant Facilities: 300 covers including Carvery section
Snack facilities: Snacks available

Racing Info

Distance raced: 250, 450, 640, 840 metres.
Track circumference: 450 metres.
Track Records: 250m Official Figure 14.98 - 10/4/98
450m August Twenty 26.70 - 1/11/97
640m El Onda 38.96 - 9/5/98
840m Musical Treat 52.45 - 15/11/97
Hare Type Outside Swaffham
Major Open Events: Golden Crest (February)

Portsmouth

General manager: Jim Snowden
Racing manager: Eric Graham
Telephone for enquiries: Enquiries 02392 698000
Email Address: jimsnowden@gralimited.co.uk
Website Address: http://www.portsmouthstadium.co.uk
Directions to track: The stadium can be seen on the left as one enters Portsmouth on the M275 motorway. Leave motorway at first slip road, at roundabout take the first junction (Twyford Avenue). About 1/2 mile turn left and follow signs to greyhound stadium. Rail: Portsmouth and Southsea Station, 5 minutes by taxi.
Race Days: Tuesday, Friday, Saturday.
Admission Prices: £4.00 including racecard.
Crowd capacity: 1,200
Car parking capacity: 300
Catering Facilities Chicken and Burger Bar providing varied menu of fast food.
Restaurant Facilities: Situated in Paddock Bar - seating for 70 people.
Snack facilities: Two snack bars offering tea, coffee, plus sandwiches, sweets etc.

Racing Info

Distance raced: 438, 610, 792, 964 metres.
Track circumference: 354 metres.
Run To First Bend: 90 metres (438m)
95 metres (610m)
Track Records: 256m Lissadell Tiger 15.55 - 09/11/89
438m Beaver Dip 26.37 - 16/12/88
610m Firmount Flapjack 38.14 - 13/10/00
792m My Texette 50.52 - 28/07/93
964m Wheres Dunait 62.94 - 28/07/93
Hare Type Inside Sumner
Major Open Events: Golden Muzzle (October)

Reading

General manager: Martyn Dore
Racing manager: Ian Sillence
Telephone for enquiries: 0118 986 3161
Email Address: readingdogs@clara.co.uk
Directions to track: Allied Presentations Ltd Reading Stadium Bennet Road Smallmead Reading RG2 0JL. M4, take junction 11, (Bennett Road 5 minutes from M4 off A33). Rail: Reading Station, five minutes by taxi to the stadium.
Race Days: Tuesday 7.35pm, Thursday 7.20pm, Saturday 7.00pm.
Admission Prices: £3.50 including racecard.
Crowd capacity: 3,500
Car parking capacity: 3,500
Catering Facilities Restaurant and fast food outlet.
Corporate Facilities: Room available for 100 maximum (buffet available).
Restaurant Facilities: 80 seats (Tel:0118 971 4325).
Snack facilities: Fast food bar.

Racing Info

Distance raced: 275, 465, 660, 850, 1045 metres.
Track circumference: 385 metres.
Run To First Bend: 80 metres (465m)
Track Records: 275m Greenfield Box 16.32 - 23/10/82
465m Blue Murlen 27.56 - 28/04/97
465mH Wisley Wonder 28.45 - 22/05/97
660m Lydpal Frankie 40.71 - 16/05/99
660mH Gold Splash 41.95 - 24/04/93
850m Lady Flyaway 53.56 - 03/05/98
1045m Souda Bay 67.58 - 03/05/98
Hare Type Outside Sumner
Major Open Events: Reading Masters (June/July)
Hunt Cup (December)

Romford

General manager: W R Hiscock

Racing manager: Peter O'Dowd

Telephone for enquiries: 01708 762345

Email Address: romford.stadium@coral.co.uk

Website Address: http://www.trap6.com/romford

Directions to track: Situated on the A118 London Road, Romford. 15 minutes from M25, junction 28 via A12. Rail: Romford Station, 5 minutes by taxi.

Race Days: Monday, Wednesday, Friday and Saturday evenings. Thursday afternoons and Saturday mornings.

Admission Prices: Main Stand: Monday & Wednesday £3.00, Friday £5.00, Saturday £5.50.

Millennium Stand: Monday & Wednesday £1.50, Friday £3.50, Saturday £4.00.

Afternoon and morning meetings free admission.

Crowd capacity: 4,300

Car parking capacity: 380 (street parking also available)

Six Pack Details: Monday, Wednesday and Friday - £10.00 Millennium Stand - £12.00 Main Stand. Saturday - £12.00 Millennium Stand - £14.00 Main Stand.

Catering Facilities Three bars in main stand. Two in Millennium and one in restaurant.

Corporate Facilities: Incorporated within restaurant and Marquee.

Restaurant Facilities: 250 covers.

Snack facilities: Two in both stands.

Racing Info

Distance raced: 225, 400, 575, 750, 925 metres.

Track circumference: 350 metres.

Run To First Bend: 67 metres (400m & 575m)

Track Records: 225m Lindas Pips 13.54 - 17/07/98

400m Sandwichsunshine 23.58 - 27/09/96

400mH Rossa Ranger 24.26 - 11/01/02
575m Palace Issue 34.81 - 09/07/99
575mH El Tenor 35.53 - 19/02/99
715m Scurlogue Champ 44.18 - 16/04/85
750m Killeacle Phoebe 46.64 - 19/06/01
925m Salina 59.13 - 07/04/81
1100m Gregagh Prince 72.59 - 10/03/87
 Hare Type Outside Swaffham
Major Open Events: Coral Golden Sprint (April)
Coral Champion Stakes (July)
Coral Puppy Cup (October)
Coral Essex Vase (December)

Rye House

General manager: Hazel Naylor
Racing manager: Suzanne Picton
Telephone for enquiries: 01992 469000
Directions to track: Take A10 to Hoddesdon and follow the A1170 towards Rye Park, go past B.R station and take second right, stadium behind public house. Rail: Rye House Station, adjacent to track, from Liverpool Street. Visitors may need to change at Broxbourne for Rye House.
Race Days: Thursday and Sunday. Sundays - 7.00pm
Admission Prices: £4.00 Adults, OAPS £2, children under 16 free.
Crowd capacity: 1,200
Car parking capacity: 250
Catering Facilities Three bars. Catering facilities and fast food.
Snack facilities: Traditional fish and chips bar.

Racing Info

Distance raced: 265, 445, 485, 630, 685, 865, 905 metres.
Track circumference: 420 metres.
Run To First Bend: 80 metres (4 bends), 40 metres (6 bends)
Track Records: 210m Our Dog Raphael 13.59 - 29/03/98
265m Mossley Mead 15.87 - 10/10/99
445m Prinz Eugen 26.34 - 06/09/98
485m Night Trooper 28.52 - 25/09/96
485mH Creevy Rover 29.56 - 20/08/00
685m Dunmurry Flight 41.75 - 11/10/95
865m Bubbly Princess 53.25 - 04/04/99
905m Souda Bay 56.58 - 29/03/98
Hare Type Swaffham McGee

Shawfield (Glasgow)

General manager: Robert Lithgow
Racing manager: Alex McTaggart
Telephone for enquiries: 0141 6474121
Fax 0141 6477265
Directions to track: Rutherglen, Lanarks., signposted from the end of M74.
Race Days: Tuesday, Thursday, Friday and Saturday evenings.
Admission Prices: £4.00
Catering Facilities Restaurant and fast food facilities

Racing Info

Distance raced: 300, 450, 480, 480H, 500, 670, 730, 882, 932 metres.
Track circumference: 432 metres.
Run To First Bend: 100 metres (300m)
90 metres (500m)
30 metres (670m)
Track Records: 300m Ravage Again 17.35 - 7/4/90
450m Fairhill Boy 26.85 - 27/10/89
480m Justright Melody 28.87 - 28/8/95
500m Droopys Sandy 29.39 - 21/5/94
500mH Face The Mutt 31.07 - 22/5/82
510mH Lovely Pud 31.63 - 9/7/84
670m Crack Of The Ash 40.50 - 11/9/93
730m Decoy Princess 45.09 - 16/8/88
882m Rosemoor Flower 56.55 - 13/04/02
932 Silken Dancer 59.35 - 2/9/93
Hare Type Swaffham
Major Open Events: Regal Scottish Derby (April)
St Mungo Cup (October)
William King Cup

Sheffield

General manager: Jon S. Carter

Racing manager: David Perry

Telephone for enquiries: 0114 234 3074

Email Address: owlerton@aol.com

Website Address: http://members.aol.com/owlerton

Directions to track: On the A61 North, next to the Hillsborough football ground (Sheffield Wednesday). From the M1 south junction 36, city centre A61 North Penistone Rd. From M1 north, junction 36 past Sheffield Wednesday on right. Rail: Midland Station, 5 minutes by taxi.

Race Days: Tuesday, Friday and Saturday evenings. Monday and Thursday afternoons.

Admission Prices: Tuesday £3.00, Friday and Saturday £5.00. Monday and Thursday free.

Crowd capacity: 4,000

Car parking capacity: 700

Six Pack Details: Tuesday, Friday and Saturday - minimum of 10.

Catering Facilities Restaurant seating 140. Hare and Hound bar. Sportsmans Tavern. Coffee Shop.

Corporate Facilities: Restaurant available

Restaurant Facilities: 140 seats - A La Carte

Snack facilities: Numerous at track

Racing Info

Distance raced: 280, 362, 480, 500, 500h, 660, 720, 800, 915, 934 metres.

Track circumference: 425 metres.

Run To First Bend: 62 metres (500m)

Track Records: 280m Parliament Act 16.38 - 22/07/00

290m Fosseway 16.77 - 27/02/99

362m Farloe Bubble 20.82 - 04/10/97

480m Reggies Hero 28.04 - 14/11/97

500m Plastercene Gem 29.00 - 08/08/98

500mH Autumn Merlin 29.94 - 04/07/00
660m Suncrest Sail 39.40 - 19/07/96
660m Droopys Rhys 39.40 - 27/11/01
720m Cherry Andy 43.44 - 27/11/01
730m Suncrest Sail 43.64 - 30/04/95
800m Hollinwood Poppy 48.25 - 27/12/00
915m Hollinwood Poppy 56.25 - 04/07/00
934m Thornfield Poppy 58.83 - 13/11/98
Hare Type Outside Swaffham
Major Open Events: William Hill Steel City Cup
Dransfield Invitation
Queen Mother Cup
Nigel Troth Yorkshire Oaks
Harry Holmes Memorial

Sittingbourne

General manager: Roger Cearns
Racing manager: Jess Packer
Telephone for enquiries: 01795 475547 (between 10am and 5pm Monday to Friday)
Racing Office: 01795 438438
Email Address: sittingbourne.dogs@cableinet.co.uk
Website Address: http://www.sittingbournegreyhounds.co.uk
Directions to track: Central Park Stadium Eurolink Sittingbourne Kent ME10 3SB.
From M2 or M20. Take A249 towards Sheerness (Junction 5 from M2, Junction 7 from M20}. Then either Take A2 exit and continue towards Sittingbourne Town Centre. Keep to left on one-way system. From Sittingbourne Station, follow signs to Central Park. or Take B2006 exit and follow signs to Sittingbourne Industry. At fourth roundabout turn right along Mill Way. Go straight over next roundabout into Eurolink Way. Go straight over next roundabout and follow signs to Central Park.
Race Days: Thursday and Saturday (7.35pm), Sunday (7pm.) Christmas period: 24 November - 29 December, nights change to Wednesdays, Fridays and Saturdays – excluding Xmas Eve and Xmas Day. Boxing Day (11am.)
Admission Prices: £4.00 including race card, Saturday £4.50, Sunday £5.00. Accompanied children under 14 have free entry.
Crowd capacity: 4,750
Car parking capacity: 1,000
Catering Facilities Restaurant, three bars, two fast food outlets
Corporate Facilities: Three superbly appointed private rooms, each holding up to 40/50 people, plus the Eurosuite - for up to 400, complete with bar, stage and dance floor. The Central Lounge caters for 180. All have excellent views of the track and CCTV. Public Entertainment licence until 1am.
Conference Facilities: 24 acres of hard and soft surfaces for outdoor

corporate events/concerts etc.

Restaurant Facilities: 180-seat trackside Eurosuite Restaurant. Tote messenger service. CCTV.

Snack facilities: Fast food bar serving burgers, chicken and chips etc. plus food counter in Central Lounge serving pot meals, jacket potatoes etc.

Racing Info

Distance raced: 265, 473, 473H, 642, 708, 916 metres.

Track circumference: 443 metres.

Track Records: 265m Fast Ranger 16.20 - 24/11/99

473m Droopys Vieri 28.53 - 26/03/00

473mH Ballmac Keano 29.41 - 01/07/01

642m Lobo 39.96 - 07/10/99

708m Sumi Girl 44.32 - 27/11/98

916m Jodie With Flex 58.29 - 14/02/99

Hare Type Outside Swaffham

Major Open Events: Kent Derby(August)

Open events every Sunday.

Stainforth (Meadow Court Stadium)

General manager: Barbara Tompkins
Racing manager: Andrew Walker and Richard Bentley
Telephone for enquiries: 01302 351639
Email Address: meadowcourt@greyhoundstadium.fsnet.co.uk
Website Address: http://www.greyhoundstadium.fsnet.co.uk
Directions to track: M18 Junction 4, A630 2 miles to A18, follow signs
to Dunsville traffic lights, turn left down the Broadway, 2 miles to
Stainforth. Rail: Doncaster Station, 8 miles. Hatfield and Stainforth local
line serving Doncaster-Rotherham-Sheffield.
Race Days: Tuesday, Friday and Saturday. First race 7.30pm.
Admission Prices: £4.50
Crowd capacity: 1,500
Car parking capacity: 500
Six Pack Details: Tuesday, Friday and Saturday.
Catering Facilities Carvery Restaurant (reservations essential) and snack
bar.
Corporate Facilities: Five executive suites.
Restaurant Facilities: 170 covers
Snack facilities: Fast food 30 seater.

Racing Info

Distance raced: 278, 480, 666, 709, 888, 925 metres.
Track circumference: 438 metres.
Run To First Bend: 105 metres (278m)
68 metres (458m)
105 metres (495m)
105 metres (709m)
Track Records: 278m Musical Chair 16.94
480m Toronto Mohawk 29.28
709m Lets Go Mika 44.91
910m Let Us Know 58.43
Hare Type Fannon/Swaffham

Sunderland (Regal Stadium)

General manager: David Maudlin
Racing manager: Jimmy Nunn
Telephone for enquiries: 0191 536 7250
Fax 0191 519 1151
Email Address: enquiries@sunderlanddogs.com
Website Address: http:// www.sunderlanddogs.com
Directions to track: The stadium is situated on the A184 between the A19 and Sunderland. From A19 South: Travel north on A19 passing Nissan factory on left-hand side. At the main roundabout ahead turn right along A184. Go through West Boldon, East Boldon. We are approximately 800 yards after the national speed limit signs (on the left hand side).
From A19 North: From Tyne Tunnel, follow A19 south until you reach Testo's roundabout. Turn left along A184. Pass through West Boldon, East Boldon. We are approximately 800 yards after the national speed limit signs (on the left hand side).
Race Days: Wednesday, Friday and Saturday evenings. Monday and Tuesday afternoons (BAGS)
Admission Prices: Adults, £5. Under 16's, free
Crowd capacity: 1,500
Car parking capacity: 500
Catering Facilities Northern lights restaurant provides an excellent view of the racing and a quality freshly prepared meal at a realistic price (seats 150). 4 bars
Corporate Facilities: 5 executive suites, function room (seats 200).

Racing Info

Distance raced: 261, 450, 640, 828, metres
Track circumference: 378 metres.
Run To First Bend: 93 metres (450m)
84 metres (640m)
Track Records: 261m Gold Buster 15.60 - 10/02/96

450m Harsu Super 27.00 - 25/10/00
640m Autumn Tiger 38.97 - 22/10/95
640m Hcp Goodnight Vienna 39.56 - 10/10/98
828m Doras Miller 52.45 - 13/02/02
Hare Type Outside McGee
Major Open Events: Regal Puppy Derby (Nov)
Regal Gold Cup (Jan)
Open puppy competition most months, regular open races

Swindon

General manager: Brian Ludgate
Racing manager: Clive Oseman
Telephone for enquiries: 01793 721 253
Email Address: sales@stadiauk.com
Website Address: http://www.swindongreyhounds.com
Directions to track: From the M4 take junction 15, follow A419 for 4-5 miles to Bunsdon, turn left at traffic lights and stadium is 100 yards on the left. Rail: Swindon Station, taxi ride to track.
Race Days: Wednesday, Friday and Saturday evenings. Thursday and Friday afternoons.
Admission Prices: £5.00. Children £1.00. Afternoon meetings free.
Crowd capacity: 2,000
Car parking capacity: 2,000
Catering Facilities 140 seater restaurant. Two snack bars. Four bars.
Corporate Facilities: Restaurant.
Restaurant Facilities: 150 covers.
Snack facilities: Two snack bars.

Racing Info

Distance raced: 285, 460, 480, 480H, 509, 685, 737 metres.
Track circumference: 452 metres.
Run To First Bend: 100 metres (509m)
Track Records: 285m Leaders Highway 16.23 - 10/06/98
460m Glideaway Flash 27.55 - 15/07/98
480m Three Wells 28.60 - 11/04/01
480mH Carnmore Prince 29.35 - 09/08/00
509m Broadacres Butch 29.85 - 04/04/01
685m Get It You 41.89 - 23/11/01
737m Top Party 45.19 - 12/12/01
Hare Type Swaffham McGee
Major Open Events: British Produce Stakes (June)

VICTOR KNIGHT

William Hill Swindon Derby (August)
Pride of the West (September)

Walthamstow (London)

General manager: N/A

Racing manager: Chris Page

Telephone for enquiries: General Enquiries: 020 8498 3300

Restaurant Bookings: 020 8498 3333

Email Address: mail@wsgreyhound.co.uk

Website Address: http://www.wsgreyhound.co.uk

Directions to track: Chingford Road, London, E4 8SJ

M11 southbound, take right hand fork at end of motorway onto A406, come off at second exit (Crooked Billet roundabout), turn right at roundabout, track 100 yards on right. A406, track can be seen to the left as Crooked Billet roundabout approaches. Take first exit on roundabout. Rail: Walthamstow Central from Liverpool Street of on Victoria Line tube. Five minutes to stadium by bus (very frequent service) or taxi.

Race Days: Tuesday, Thursday and Saturday evenings. Monday and Friday afternoons.

Admission Prices: £3.00 Popular enclosure (Tuesdays free), £6.00 Main enclosure. Monday and Friday lunchtimes free admission and half price drinks (please check times).

Crowd capacity: 5,000

Car parking capacity: 1,000

Six Pack Details: Tuesday, Thursday and Saturday - no minimum numbers.

Catering Facilities 2 main restaurants - The famous Paddock Grill and The Stowaway Grill.

American Diner (Six-pack meals served here).

Six bars.

Various fast food and tea bars.

Corporate Facilities: Facilities include four corporate boxes, which are available Monday and Friday lunchtimes (discounted) and all evening meetings.

Conference Facilities: Facilities are available on request.

Restaurant Facilities: Paddock Grill and Stowaway (Mid-week moneysaver deals in the Stowaway for the family night out - ring 0208 498 3333 for more details).

Snack facilities: American Classic Diner and Punters. Several tea bars.

Racing Info

Distance raced: 415, 435, 475, 640, 840, 880, 1,045 metres.

Track circumference: 405 metres.

Run To First Bend: 100 metres (475m)

68 metres (640m)

Track Records: 415m Kilmacsimon Wave 24.88 - 14/09/95

435m Union Decree 25.71 - 19/11/98

475m Star Of Tyrone 28.49 - 19/03/95

475m Westmead Chick 28.49 - 11/06/95

475mH Glown Fox28.92 - 06/06/97

640m Spring Rose 39.05 - 05/10/96

640mH El Tenor 40.39 - 09/03/99

820m Long Island Jim 51.50 - 02/11/95

840m Redwood Sara 52.12 - 07/08/97

880m Decoy Lynx 55.65 - 08/10/94

1045m Handy Score 67.90 - 19/11/98

Hare Type Swaffham

Major Open Events: The UK Packaging Arc (February/March)

The Victor Chandler Grand Prix (September/October)

Racing Post Festival (mid-November).

Wimbledon (London)

General manager: Mick Hardy

Racing manager: Simon Harris

Telephone for enquiries: 020 8946 8000

Email Address: wmraceoffice@gralimited.co.uk

Website Address: http://www.wimbledonstadium.co.uk

Directions to track: A219, turn left at Alexandra Road and across traffic lights into Plough Lane, stadium on the left. Rail: Tooting Broadway (Northern Line), Wimbledon (from Waterloo Station or on District Line), Earlsfield (from Waterloo).

Race Days: Tuesday, Friday & Saturday evenings, doors open 6.30pm, first race 7.30pm.

Admission Prices: Grandstand £5.50.

Mick The Miller Stand £4.00.

Crowd capacity: 6,000

Car parking capacity: 900

Six Pack Details: Tuesday, Friday and Saturday - minimum of 10.

Catering Facilities Fast food areas. Four executive suites. Two Restaurants. Buffet facilities. Bar facilities.

Corporate Facilities: Four Executive Boxes - a first class venue which combines with superb entertainment. The air-conditioned, glass-fronted suites provide an excellent trackside view as they are situated on the finishing straight. Each suite has its own tote betting service, a fully equipped bar and a team of trained staff, who are on hand to ensure a personal and professional service is provided.

Conference Facilities: The Boardroom

The Diamond Room

Restaurant Facilities: The Star Attraction - a silver service restaurant with tiered seating overlooking the start to finish line offering a superb three-course meal whilst enjoying the racing. The Broadway Restaurant - an informal restaurant, situated behind the starting boxes offering a three-course meal in a fun, lively environment.

Snack facilities: Bar snacks crisps etc.

Racing Info

Distance raced: 252, 460, 480, 660, 680, 868, 1068 metres.
Track circumference: 408 metres.
Run To First Bend: 100 metres (460m & 480m)
70 metres (660m)
Track Records: 252m Slipaway Jaydee 14.95 - 16/03/94
272m Dynamic Fair 16.11 - 28/06/97
460m Double Bid - 25/06/88
460mH Arfur Daley 27.80 - 20/03/93
480m Greenane Squire 28.21 - 12/07/94
660m First Defence 40.12 - 08/03/94
660mH Gold Splash 41.15 - 2/08/94
680m Geinis Champion 41.73 - 24/06/95
820m Sail On Valerie 51.16 - 30/12/89
Chestnut Beauty 51.16 - 21/04/93
868m Sandy Lane 54.11 - 06/05/83.
Hare Type Outside Swaffham
Major Open Events: Racing Post Juvenile (January)
William Hill Springbok (February)
William Hill Grand National (March)
William Hill Greyhound Derby (June)
William Hill Puppy Derby (September)
TV Trophy (October)
William Hill Puppy Oaks (November)
William Hill St Leger (November)
William Hill Oaks (December)

Yarmouth

General manager: Simon Franklin
Racing manager: Stephen Franklin
Telephone for enquiries: 01493 720343
Email Address: shaun.yarmouthstadium@virgin.net
Website Address: http://www.yarmouthstadium.co.uk
Directions to track: From Norwich take the A47 to Great Yarmouth.
Once in Great Yarmouth follow the brown signs to Yarmouth Stadium.
Rail: Yarmouth Station (from Norwich). Stadium short taxi ride away.
Race Days: Monday, Wednesday and Saturday evenings. Boxing Day
morning (10.30pm) New Years Day (7.30pm)
Admission Prices: £5.00 adults, £4.00 OAP's. Accompanied children
under 16 free.
Crowd capacity: 5,804
Car parking capacity: 1,000 - 50p per car.
Six Pack Details: Monday, Wednesday and Saturday - minimum of 10.
Catering Facilities Raceview Diner with own seating. Area for the best
in bar food.
Corporate Facilities: Executive Lounge overlooking winning line.
Seating for up to 70 guests.
Restaurant Facilities: None
Snack facilities: Ground floor, small bar, fast food.

Racing Info

Distance raced: 277, 462, 659, 843 metres.
Track circumference: 382 metres.
Run To First Bend: 85 metres (462m)
Track Records: 277m Respect 16.50 - 16/08/00
462m Dempsey Duke 27.68 - 19/09/99
659m Big City 40.79 - 24/09/88
843m Change Guard 53.62 - 25/08/86
1041m Some Moth 68.81 - 08/12/90

Hare Type Swaffham
Major Open Events: The Wafcol East Anglian Challenge (August)
The East Anglian Greyhound Derby (September)
The Pepsi Cola Sprint (September)
Bass Charrington Brewers Cup
KFC Graded 100

Ireland

BALLYSKEAGH

Ballyskeagh Greyhound Stadium,
Ballyskeagh Road,
Lambeg,
Lisburn,
Co. Antrim.
Manager : Mr. Charles Keown
Telephone : 0801 232 616720
Race Nights : Monday, Friday & Saturday 8.00pm
Distances : 375 yds., 525 yds., 550 yds., 575 yds., 600 yds., 880 yds.
Track Records :

375 yds.	PRIME LOCATION	11-06-99	19.89
525 yds.	DUAL BLACK	27-10-97	28.48
550 yds.	DUFFYS KESTREL	12-12-97	29.85
575 yds.	DUFFYS KESTREL	23-10-98	31.53
600 yds.	CHESTERS CHOICE	27-06-97	32.46
880 yds.	MADE OF SESKIN	07-03-97	49.98

CORK

Curraheen Park,
Curraheen Road,
Bishopstown,
Co. Cork.
Racing & General Manager : Mr. Noel Holland
Marketing & Commercial Manager : Mr. Fergal Keniry
Telephone : 021 – 4543095
Email :info@Curraheenpark.igb.ie
Race Nights : Wednesday, Thursday & Saturday 8.00pm
Distances : 300 yds., 500 yds., 525 yds., 700 yds., 745 yds.
Track Records :

300 yds.	SARAS MOTH	23-09-89	16.35
500 yds.	CASTLELYONS ICE	08-10-94	27.88
525 yds.	LIVE CONTENDER	17-11-90	28.50
700 yds.	KILCOMMON CROSS	04-06-90	39.70
	ALWAYS GOOD	13-05-95	39.70
745 yds.	MATCHLESS MATT	07-07-93	42.78

DERRY

Derry Greyhound Stadium,
Brandywell Grounds,
Derry.
Manager : Mr. Michael McLoughlin
Telephone : 0801 504 265461
Race Nights : Monday & Friday 8.00pm
Distances : 300 yds., 500 yds., 525 yds., 600 yds., 720 yds.
Track Records :

300 yds.	PIPERS GOLD	22-09-89	16.43
500 yds.	CENTRAL SUPREME	24-08-90	27.85
525 yds.	WESTPARK CITY	15-06-84	29.04

| 600 yds. | HOMEFIELD KING | 01-11-91 | 33.92 |
| 720 yds. | MISS JAHOUSKY | 16-08-85 | 41.20 |

DUNDALK

Dundealgan Greyhound Race Company,
The Ramparts,
Dundalk,
Co. Louth.
Manager : Mr. John McComish
Telephone : 042 - 34113
Race Nights : Monday & Saturday 8.00pm
Distances : 320 yds., 500 yds., 525 yds., 550 yds., 760 yds.
Track Records :

320 yds.	BOYNE WALK	15-08-93	17.46
500 yds.	BIG CYRIL	15-08-93	27.92
525 yds.	SUMMERHILL GIFT	15-08-93	29.14
550 yds.	SUMMERHILL GIFT	17-07-93	30.64
760 yds.	RATIFY	15-08-93	43.44

DUNGANNON

Oaks Park Greyhound Stadium,
Dungannon,
Co. Tyrone.
Manager : Mr. Dave Bill
Telephone : 0801 868 722023
Race Nights : Wednesday & Friday 8.00pm
Distances : 325 yds., 500 yds., 525 yds., 550 yds., 780 yds.
Track Records :

325 yds.	CASSIE BOY	05-02-92	17.25
500 yds.	SPEEDY SHANE	07-07-99	27.08
525 yds.	GEMS WHISPER	29-04-92	28.65
550 yds.	GLENHILL PRIDE	09-10-91	29.75
780 yds.	BRACCAN CONNIE	09-10-91	43.94

ENNISCORTHY

Enniscorthy Greyhound Race Company,
Showgrounds,
Enniscorthy,
Co. Wexford.
Manager : Mr. Stephen Cullen
Telephone : 054 - 33172
Race Nights : Monday & Thursday 8.00pm
Distances : 350 yds., 525 yds., 550 yds., 600 yds., 830 yds. 1,005 yds.
Track Records :

350 yds.	LUGGERS SPEEDY	01-09-94	18.57
525 yds.	MICHAELS MACHINE	11-11-93	28.92
550 yds.	KILCLONEY CHIEF	19-07-93	30.22
600 yds.	SPIT IT OUT	21-09-95	33.01
830 yds.	TONDUFF SUSIE	03-11-94	47.32
1,005 yds.	ALMOST DASHING	05-05-97	59.60

GALWAY (Closed for renovation)

Galway Greyhound Race Company,
College Road,
Galway
Manager : Mr. Tom Moran
Telephone : 091 - 562273
Race Nights : Tuesday & Friday 8.00pm
Distances : 325 yds., 525 yds., 550 yds., 810 yds., 525 yds. Hurdles.
Track Records :

325 yds.	DAMERS VALLEY	26-07-99	17.57
525 yds.	NO ROAD BACK	28-07-97	29.05
550 yds.	VINTAGE PRINCE	15-08-97	30.28
810 yds.	CLYDAL PAL	04-08-95	46.25
525 yds	H. CHUMS CHOICE	24-07-98	29.71
	ROCKET MERLIN	30-07-99	29.71

HAROLDS CROSS

Dublin Greyhound & Sports Association,
Harolds Cross,
Dublin 6W.
Commercial Manager : Mr. Pat O'Donovan
Racing Manager : Mr. Eamonn Mackie
Telephone : 01 – 4973439
Race Nights : Monday, Tuesday, Friday 8.00pm
Distances : 330 yds., 525 yds., 550 yds., 580 yds., 750 yds., 830 yds.,
1,025 yds.
Track Records :

330 yds.	QUARTER TO FIVE	09-04-99	17.52
525 yds.	PRINCE TINRAH	02-10-98	28.50
550 yds.	BARNEYS ALARM	02-08-91	30.20
580 yds.	TRACEYS TRIUMPH	06-10-95	31.68
750 yds.	AZURI	24-06-83	42.00
830 yds.	BROOKDALE LADY	23-06-95	46.72
1,025 yds.	BODIES LISA	04-12-92	59.52

KILKENNY

Kilkenny Greyhound Race Company,
St. James Park,
Kilkenny.
Manager : Mr. John O'Flynn
Telephone : 056 - 21214
Race Nights : Wednesday & Friday 8.00pm
Distances : 300 yds., 525 yds., 700 yds., 745 yds.
Track Records :

300 yds.	MAGIC SIZZLER	04-06-99	16.23
525 yds.	SPIRAL NIKITA	07-07-96	28.70
700 yds.	DEENSIDE MIST	05-07-91	40.47
745 yds.	SUMMERHILL SWIFT	06-07-97	43.50

LIFFORD

Lifford Greyhound Race Company,
Lifford,
Co. Donegal
Manager : Mr. Cathal Magee
Telephone : 074 – 41083
Race Nights : Thursday & Saturday 8.00pm
Distances : 325 yds., 525 yds., 550 yds., 575 yds., 790 yds.
Track Records :

325 yds.	PATS GALE	17-08-96	17.54
525 yds.	AILSA CARMEL	02-07-94	28.78
550 yds.	AILSA CARMEL	06-08-94	30.22
575 yds.	DRUMSNA ISLE	22-08-99	31.72
790 yds.	BARRACK MAID	17-08-78	45.03

LIMERICK

Limerick Greyhound Race Company,
Markets Field,
Limerick.
General Manager : Mr. Gus Ryan
Telephone : 061 – 475170
Race Nights : Monday, Thursday & Saturday 8.00pm
Distances : 300 yds., 525 yds., 550 yds., 700 yds., 750 yds.
Track Records :

300 yds.	CLON FLASH	19-08-96	16.26
525 yds.	DEEP DECISION	31-05-97	28.37
550 yds.	FRISBY FLASHING	16-10-99	29.64
700 yds.	ONE MORE STOP	16-10-99	39.06
750 yds.	KILLEAGH KING	17-05-97	42.54

LONGFORD

Longford Sports Limited,
Park Road,
Longford.
Manager :
Telephone : 044 – 46441
Race Nights : Monday & Friday 8.00pm
Distances : 330 yds., 525 yds., 550 yds.
Track Records :

330 yds.	COOL CANUCK	04-06-99	18.02
525 yds.	PEPSI PRINCESS	01-09-89	28.82
550 yds.	PEPSI PETE	19-07-93	30.32

MULLINGAR

Mullingar Greyhound Race Company,
Ballinderry,
Mullingar,
Co. Westmeath.
Telephone : 044 – 48348
Race Nights : Tuesday & Saturday 8.00pm
Distances : 325 yds., 525 yds., 550 yds., 600 yds., 805 yds.
Track Records :

325 yds.	SWIFT MANX	21-09-99	18.28
525 yds.	UNSINKABLE GIRL	02-10-99	28.88
550 yds.	UNSINKABLE GIRL	21-08-99	30.66
600 yds.	SPRINGWILL DAN	05-10-96	33.44
805 yds.	MORAL PARK	22-08-92	46.74

NEWBRIDGE

Newbridge Greyhound Race Company,
Newbridge,
Co. Kildare.
Manager : Mr. Billy Bell
Telephone : 045 - 431270
Race Nights : Monday & Friday 8.00pm
Distances : 300 yds., 525 yds., 550 yds., 600 yds., 750 yds., 820 yds.
Track Records :

300 yds.	KILQUAIN MELODY	02-07-99	16.36
525 yds.	JUDICIAL PRIDE	14-06-99	28.58
550 yds.	DROOPYS MOSSIE	03-07-94	29.96
600 yds.	GUESS TWICE	28-06-91	32.86
750 yds.	LOCH BO ANCHOR	03-07-94	42.34
820 yds.	STRONG CHOICE	17-07-92	46.84

SHELBOURNE PARK

Shelbourne Greyhound Stadium,
Shelbourne Park,
Dublin 4.
Managing Director : Mr. Noel Hynes
General Manager : Mr. Paddy Ryan
Telephone : 01 – 6683502
Website: www.shelbournepark.com
Race Nights : Wednesday, Thursday & Saturday 8.00pm
Distances : 360 yds., 525 yds., 550 yds., 575 yds., 600 yds., 750 yds., 1,025 yds., 525 yds. Hurdles.
Track Records :

360 yds.	UPPER SPARK	25-05-96	19.05
525 yds.	CHART KING	03-04-99	28.40
550 yds.	FRISBY FLASHING	30-12-99	29.89
575 yds.	DREAM ON LADY	17-07-99	31.57
	MOUNTAYLOR BAY	04-09-99	31.57
600 yds.	KILMESSAN JET	24-04-99	32.58

750 yds.	GET CONNECTED	10-10-98	42.01
1,025 yds.	RUSCAR DANA	06-08-88	59.91
525 yds.	H. KILDARE SLIPPY	03-10-88	29.18

THURLES

Thurles Greyhound Race Company,
Townpark,
Thurles,
Co.Tipperary
Racing Manager : Mr.Brian Collins
Telephone : 0504 – 21003
Race Nights : Tuesday & Saturday 8.00pm
Distances : 330 yds., 525 yds., 550 yds., 575 yds., 840 yds.
Track Records :

330 yds.	QUARTER TO FIVE	11-05-99	17.64
525 yds.	AIRMOUNT ROVER	01-05-99	28.92
550 yds.	EMLY EXPRESS	21-07-96	30.18
575 yds.	DEENSIDE LION	23-05-98	31.73
840 yds.	GLENGALL STAR	21-08-93	47.62

TRALEE

Kingdom Greyhound Stadium,
Oakview Park,
Tralee,
Co. Kerry
Racing Manager : Mr.John Ward
Marketing Manager : Mr.Rory Kerins
Telephone : 066 - 24033
Race Nights : Tuesday & Friday 8.00pm
Distances : 325 yds., 500 yds., 525 yds., 550 yds., 570 yds., 750 yds.
Track Records :

325 yds.	PINEAPPLE MANDY	23-04-99	17.46
500 yds.	FLYING RIO	20-03-98	27.74
525 yds.	ROCKING BOB	29-08-97	28.41

550 yds.	CAPE PRINCE	28-07-95	29.78
570 yds.	WISE COMMANDER	26-09-96	31.14
750 yds.	EASTER TIDINGS	25-05-99	42.15

WATERFORD

Waterford Greyhound Race Company,
Kilcohan Park,
Waterford.
Manager : Mr. Michael Higgins
Telephone : 051 – 874531
Race Nights : Wednesday & Saturday 7.50pm
Distances : 300 yds., 500 yds., 525 yds., 550 yds., 730 yds.
Track Records :

300 yds.	QUARTER TO FIVE	03-07-99	15.99
500 yds.	KILDALLON EDDIE	19-08-98	27.68
525 yds.	MR. PICKWICK	24-05-97	28.25
550 yds.	SINEADS ROCKET	08-05-99	29.74
730 yds.	SUMMERHILL SWIFT	24-05-97	40.68

YOUGHAL

Youghal Greyhound Race Company,
Youghal,
Co. Cork.
Manager : Mr. Finbar Coleman
Telephone : 024 - 92305
Race Nights : Tuesday & Friday 8.00pm
Distances: 325 yds., 525 yds., 550 yds., 700 yds.
Track Records :

325 yds.	LEMON CLOVER	18-10-96	17.34
525 yds.	GOLD SPITFIRE	22-08-97	28.80
550 yds.	BORNA BEST	09-05-97	29.94
700 yds.	GAYTIME BLONDE	29-08-97	39.36

United States of America

ALABAMA

The Birmingham Race Course
(Jefferson County Racing Association)
1000 John Rogers Drive
Birmingham, AL 35210
(205) 838-7500
General Manager: Joe O'Neil
General Months of Operation: Year-round
www.birminghamracecourse.com

Mobile Greyhound Park
Post Office Box 43
Theodore, Alabama 36590-0043
(334) 653-5000
General Manager: David Jones
General Months of Operation: Year-round
www.mobilegreyhoundpark.com

VictoryLand
(Macon County Greyhound Park, Inc.)
Post Office Box 128
Shorter, Alabama 36075-0128
(334) 727-0540
General Manager: James Baker
General Months of Operation: Year-round
www.victoryland.com

ARIZONA

Apache Greyhound Park
(American Greyhound Racing, Inc.)
2551 West Apache Trail
Apache Junction, Arizona 85220
(602) 982-2371
General Manager: Edward C. Braunger
General Months of Operation: November-April
www.phoenixgreyhoundpark.com

Phoenix Greyhound Park
(American Greyhound Racing, Inc.)
3801 East Washington Street
Phoenix, Arizona 85034-1796
(602)-273-7181
General Manager: Daniel A. Luciano
General Months of Operation: Year-round
www.phoenixgreyhoundpark.com

Tucson Greyhound Park
2601 S. 3rd Avenue
Tucson, Arizona 85713
(520) 884-7576
General Manager: Kip Keefer
President: Robert Consolo
General Months of Operation: Year-round
www.tucdogtrack.com

ARKANSAS

Southland Greyhound Park
Southland Racing Corp
PO Box 2088
West Memphis, Arkansas 72303
(870) 735-3670   1-800-467-6182
General Manager: Barry Baldwin
General Months of Operation: Year-round
www.southlandgreyhound.com

COLORADO

Cloverleaf Kennel Club
PO Box 88
Loveland, Colorado 80539
(970) 667-6211
General Manager: Joe Pardi
General Months of Operation:
Mid-February to Mid-June

Mile High Greyhound Park
Wembley USA
6200 Dahlia Street
Commerce City, Colorado
(303) 288-1591
General Manager: Steve Rose
General Months of Operation:
Mid-June to Mid February
www.wembleyusa.com/milehigh

Pueblo Greyhound Park
Wembley USA
PO Box 2220
Pueblo, Colorado 81005-2220
(719) 566-0370 or
(303) 288-1591 (Off-Season, Mile High)
General Manager: Jim Gartland
General Months of Operation: January – March

CONNECTICUT

Plainfield Greyhound Park, Inc.
Post Office Box 205
Plainfield, Connecticut 06374-0205
(203) 564-3391
General Manager: Karen Keelan
General Months of Operation: Year-round
www.trackinfo.com/pl

Shoreline Star Greyhound Park
Bridgeport Jai Alai, Inc.
255 Kossuth Street
Bridgeport, Connecticut 06088
(203) 576-1976
General Manager: Steve Alford
General Months of Operation: April – September
www.Shorelinestar.com

FLORIDA

Daytona Beach Kennel Club
Post Office Box 11470
Daytona Beach, Florida 32120
(904) 252-6484
General Manager: Harry J. Olsen
General Months of Operation: Year-round
www.dbkenneclub.com

Ebro Greyhound Park
6558 Dog Track Road
Ebro, Florida 32437
(850) 535-4048
General Manager: Stockton Hess
General Months of Operation: January – October
www.ebrogreyhoundpark.com

Flagler Greyhound Track
(West Flagler Associates, Ltd.)
Post Office Box 350940
Miami, Florida 33135-0940
(305) 649-3000
General Manager: William Hutchinson
General Months of Operation: June - Nov
(Simulcast rest of year)
www.flaglerdogs.com

Hollywood Greyhound Park
831 N. Federal Highway
Hallandale, Florida 33009
(954) 924-3200
General Manager: Dan Adkins
Director of Operations: Jerry Adkins

General Months of Operation: December - May
(Simulcast rest of year)
www.hollywoodgreyhound.com

Jefferson County Kennel Club, Inc.
PO Box 400
Monticello, Florida 32345
(850) 997-2561
President & CEO: Steve Andris
General Months of Operation:Year-round

Jacksonville Kennel Club, Inc.
Post Office Box 54249
Jacksonville, Florida 32245-4249
(904) 646-0001
General Manager: Howard I. Korman
General Months of Operation: May-September
(Simulcast rest of year)
www.jaxkennel.com

Melbourne Greyhound Park
1100 Wickham Road
Melbourne, Florida 32935
(407) 259-9800
General Manager:Patrick T.Biddix
General Months of Operation:Year-round

Orange Park Kennel Club, Inc.
Post Office Box 54249
Jacksonville, Florida 32245-4249
(904) 646-0001
General Manager: Howard I. Korman
General Months of Operation: November - April (Live)
(Simulcast rest of year)

Naples-Fort Myers Greyhound Track
(Bonita-Fort Myers Corporation)
Post Office Box 2567
Bonita Springs, Florida 33959-2567
(941) 992-2411
General Manager: William Hutchinson
General Months of Operation: Year-round
www.naplesfortmyersdogs.com/home.cfm

Palm Beach Kennel Club
(Investment Corporation of Palm Beach)
1111 North Congress Avenue
West Palm Beach, Florida 33409-6317
(561) 683-2222
General Manager: Arthur Laughlin
General Months of Operation: Year-round
www.pbkennelclub.com

Pensacola Greyhound Track, Inc.
Post Office Box 12824
Pensacola, Florida 32575-2824
(850) 445-8595
General Manager: Nicholai Schlikin
General Months of Operation: Year-round
www.pensacolagreyhoundpark.com/index2.html

St. Petersburg Kennel Club, Inc.
Derby Lane
10490 Gandy Boulevard
St. Petersburg, Florida 33702-2395
(727) 576-1361
General Manager: Vey O. Weaver
General Months of Operation: January – June
www.derbylane.com

St. Johns Greyhound Park
(Bayard Raceways, Inc.)
P.O. Box 54249
Jacksonville, Florida 32245-4249
(904) 646-0001
General Manager: Howard I. Korman
General Months of Operation:
Simulcast Only Year-round

Sarasota Kennel Club, Inc.
5400 Bradenton Road
Sarasota, Florida 34234-2999
(941) 355-7744
Track Manager: Jack Collins
General Months of Operation: January - April (Simulcast rest of Year)
www.floridagreyhoundracing.com

Sanford-Orlando Kennel Club, Inc.
Box 520280
Longwood, Florida 32752-0280
(407) 831-1600
Track Manager: Jack Collins
General Months of Operation:
November through early May
www.floridagreyhoundracing.com

Tampa Greyhound Track
(Associated Outdoor Clubs, Inc.)
Post Office Box 8096
Tampa, Florida 33674-8096
(813) 932-4313 or (813) 932-4314
General Manager: John M. "Mike" Hater
General Months of Operation: July – December
www.tampadogs.com

IOWA

Dubuque Greyhound Park
Dubuque Racing Association, Ltd.
PO Box 3190
Dubuque, Iowa 52004-3190
(319) 582-3647 1-800-373-3647
General Manager: Bruce Wentworth
General Months of Operation: May - October
(Simulcasting & Casino Operations Year-round)
Dubuque
www.dgpc.com

Bluffs Run Casino
2701 23rd Avenue
Council Bluffs, IA 51501
(712) 323-2500
General Manager: Verne Welch
General Months of Operation: Year-round
www.bluffsdogs.com

KANSAS

Wichita Greyhound Track
Post Office Box 277
Valley Center, KS 67147
(316) 755-4000
General Manager: Kip Keefer
General Months of Operation: Year-round
www.wgpi.com

The Woodlands
P.O. Box 12036
Kansas City, KS 66112
(913) 299-9797
General Manager: August J. Masciotra
General Months of Operation: Year-round

MASSACHUSETTS

Wonderland Greyhound Park
190 VFW Parkway
Revere, Massachusetts 02151
(781) 284-1300
Asst. G.M./Simulcast Director: Ron Wohlen
General Months of Operation: Year-round
www.wonderlandgreyhound.com

Raynham Taunton Greyhound Park
PO Box Box 172
Raynham, Massachusetts 02767
(508) 824-4071
Director of Operations: Kelly Carney
Director of Simulcasting: Gary Temple
www.rtgp.com

NEW HAMPSHIRE

Lakes Region Greyhound Park
N.H. Gaming Association, Ltd.
PO Box 280
Belmont, New Hampshire 03220
(603) 267-7778
General Manager: Allan E. Hart
General Months of Operation: June – September

Hinsdale Greyhound Park
Route 119
Hinsdale, New Hampshire 03451
(603) 336-5382
President: Joseph E. Sullivan III
Operations Manager:
Marcus J. Worden
www.hinsdalegreyhound.com

Seabrook Greyhound Park
(Yankee Greyhound Racing, Inc.)
P. O. Box 219
Seabrook, NH 03874-0219
603-474-3065
General Manager: Joseph Carney
General Months of Operation: Year-round
www.seabrookgreyhoundpark.com

OREGON

Multnomah Greyhound Park
(Multnomah Kennel Club, Inc.)
Post Office Box 9
Fairview, Oregon 97024-0009
(503) 667-7700 Fax: (503) 669-2124
General Manager: Carl L. Wilson
General Months of Operation: May – October
www.ez2winmgp.com

RHODE ISLAND

Lincoln Greyhound Park
1600 Louisquisset Pike
Lincoln, Rhode Island 02865-4506
(401) 723-3200
General Manager: Dan Bucci
General Months of Operation: Year-round
www.lincolnparkri.com

TEXAS

Corpus Christi Greyhound Track
(Corpus Christi Greyhound Racing Association, Ltd.)
Post Office Box 9087
Corpus Christi, Texas 78469
(361) 289-9333
General Manager: Jacques Triplett
General Months of Operation: Year-round
www.corpuschristidogs.com

Gulf Greyhound Park
1000 FM 2004, LaMarque, TX 77568
(409) 986-9500
General Manager: Barry L. Sevedge
General Months of Operation: Year-round
www.gulfgreyhound.com

Valley Race Park
2601 S. Ed Carey Dr.
Harlingen, TX 78552
(956) 412-7223
General Manager: Robert L. Bork
General Months of Operation: Year-round

WEST VIRGINIA

Wheeling Downs
1 South Stone Street
Wheeling, West Virginia 26003
(304) 232-5050
President and General Manager: Hayes Taylor
General Months of Operation: Year-round
www.wheelingdowns.com

Tri-State Greyhound Park
1 Greyhound Drive
Cross Lanes, West Virginia 25313
(304) 776-1000
General Manager: Gary Burdett
Director of Marketing: Cathy Brackbill
General Months of Operation: Year-round
http://tristategreyhound.casinocity.com/

WISCONSIN

Dairyland Greyhound Park
5522 104th Avenue
Kenosha, Wisconsin 53144
(414) 657-8200 or (800) 233-3357
General Manager: William O. Apgar, Jr.
General Months of Operation: Year-round
www.dairylandgreyhoundpark.com

Geneva Lakes Kennel Club
Post Office Box 650, 1600 E. Geneva Street
Delavan, Wisconsin 53115
(414) 728-8000 or (800) 477-4552
General Manager: Milt Roth

General Months of Operation: Year-round
www.genevagreyhounds.com

St. Croix Meadows Greyhound Racing

2200 Carmichael Road
Post Office Box 750
Hudson, Wisconsin 54016
(715) 386-6800
General Manager: Ron Geier
General Months of Operation: Year-round
www.stcroixgreyhounds.com

Reference Sources

Web Sites

Greyhound Racing is extremely well served by the World Wide Web. This is just a selection of sites from around the world that all have many links elsewhere.

United Kingdom

www.thedogs.co.uk (Official site of the British Greyhound Racing Board)

www.24dogs.com (Broadcasts live greyhound racing via webcam)

www.greyhoundsmonthly.co.uk (Monthly greyhound magazine)

www.racingpost.co.uk (Daily racing newspaper with excellent greyhound coverage)

www.trap6.com (Greyhound racing news and information)

www.ugo4u.co.uk (Union of Greyhound owners)

www.greyhoundstar.com (Online and print greyhound newspaper)

www.trapfour.co.uk (Greyhound and dog racing news, chat and gossip)

www.greyhoundrescue.co.uk (international & national information)

www.gobarkingmad.com (24/7 greyhound racing channel)

www.greyhoundpredictor.com (a real-time greyhound racing tipping tool)

www.globalgreyhounds.com (International discussion and news forum)

United States

www.racing-world.com (Links to lots of USA tracks)

www.agtoa.com (Site of the American Greyhound Track Operators Association – links to many other sites) www.texasgreyhoundassociation.com (Site of Texas greyhound organisation, huge number of links)

www.rosnet2000.com (Very comprehensive site all about greyhound racing)

www.ngagreyhounds.com (Official registry of Greyhounds in North America)

http://greybase.com/index.asp (The American Racing Greyhound Database)

www.gra-america.org (Greyhound Racing Association of America)

Ireland

www.igb.ie/(index.htm) (Site of the Irish Greyhound Racing Board – Bord na gCon)

www.sportingpress.ie (Web based racing newspaper, plenty of greyhound coverage)

Australia and New Zealand

www.anzga.org.au (Site of the Australia and New Zealand Greyhound Association Incorperated – links to the different governing bodies in these two countries plus many other sites)

www.greyhoundform.com.au (Greyhound newspaper carrying form, tips and news)

www.australiangreyhoundmagazine.com

www.nzgra.org.nz (New Zealand Greyhound Racing Association)

Books

When it comes to books about betting on greyhound racing, the sport is very poorly served. In fact if you have a computer go to the site for Amazon books and do a search on greyhound racing. The response is extremely disappointing. Of the few books that are available, almost all are US based which, although very interesting, do not always translate that well to racing in Great Britain and Ireland. Here is a very small selection with the country the text is based on in brackets:

Win at Greyhound Racing (Great Britain) by H Edwards Clarke. New edition March 2003, ISBN 1 84344 000 8

Greyhound Racing (Great Britain) by Statistician, 1991, Foulsham, ISBN 0 572 01696 4

Winner's Guide-Greyhound Racing (USA) by Prof. Jones, 1993, Cardoza Publishing, ISBN 0 94068 576 0

Greyhound Racing Annual 2003 (Great Britain) ed Jonathan Hobbs ISBN 1 90431 707 3

High Stakes Bookshop, 21 Great Ormond St, London WC1N 3JB (www.highstakes.co.uk) T: 020 7430 1021 carry a full range of books on greyhounds

HIGH STAKES PUBLISHING NEW TITLES & STOCK LIST

Qty	Title	Author	Pub Date	Price
____	Forecasting Methods for Horseracing	Peter May	Available	£14.99
____	The Education of a Poker Player	Herbert O Yardley	Available	£9.99
____	Football Fortunes	Bill Hunter	Aug '03	£9.99
____	Greyhound Racing to Win	Victor Knight	Jan '03	£9.99
____	Total Poker	David Spanier	Available	£9.99
____	Win at Greyhound Racing	H Edwards Clarke	Mar '03	£9.99
____	The Science of Winning	Burton P Fabricand	Available	£14.99
____	Profitable Football Betting	P N Steele	Available	£29.95
____	Placepot Annual: National Hunt 2002	Malcolm Boyle	Available	£9.99
____	Placepot Annual: Flat 2003	Malcolm Boyle	Mar '03	£9.99
____	Phantoms of the Card Table	David Britland	Feb '03	£25
____	Betting to Win	Prof L V Williams	Available	£25

Customer Name: . . . .

Address: . . . .

. . . .

. . . .

Order Number: . . . . **Date:** . . . . . .

Credit Card Number: . . . .

Expiry Date: . . . .

High Stakes Publishing, 21 Great Ormond St, London, WC1N 3JB, ENGLAND

T: 020 7430 1021 F: 020 7430 0021 orders@highstakes.co.uk

Please add 10% P&P for UK orders, 15% elsewhere.

Visa, Mastercard, Switch, Delta accepted.

Cheques in £Sterling, drawn on UK bank and payable to: High Stakes

For a full range of books on all aspects of gambling go to: **www.highstakes.co.uk**

or contact High Stakes Bookshop at the above address for a FREE catalogue